Edward R. Canda
Editor

Spirituality in Social Work: New Directions

Spirituality in Social Work: New Directions has been co-published simultaneously as *Social Thought*, Volume 18, Number 2 1998.

Pre-publication
REVIEWS,
COMMENTARIES,
EVALUATIONS . . .

More pre-publication
REVIEWS, COMMENTARIES, EVALUATIONS . . .

"In our attempt to quantify the unquantifiable we have deserted ourselves, the core nature of who we are as human beings: our creative and spiritual selves! It is time to correct the mistake. Ed Canda and his associates are on the good way toward that goal!

This text is a most-needed addition to training programs associated with helping professions. Its major strengths are the scope of information and the ability of all contributing authors to give practical dimension to the 'invisible dimension' of our being."

Dada M. Maglajlic, PhD
Associate Professor
Bemidji State University
& Organizing Director
IUC Dubrovnik School
of S.W. Theory & Practice

"At last the social work profession has a text that deals with the latest issues regarding religion and spirituality in social work practice. Edited by Edward Canda, foremost social work and spirituality scholar and researcher, *Spirituality in Social Work: New Directions* attempts to answer the question the social work profession has been grappling with of how to address spirituality in ways that honor spiritual diversity. . . .

As a faculty member who annually teaches a class on religion and spirituality, this book will definitely be a required text for my students. Also, essays fro this book can be used in several of the social work sequences: practice, human behavior, and policy. Ultimately, *Spirituality in Social Work: New Directions* provides knowledge and guidance for faculty who are trying to respond to the Council on Social Work Education curriculum guidelines that indicate religious diversity and spirituality should be addressed along with other forms of human diversity and for practitioners who are confronted with their clients' spiritual and religious diversity on a daily basis."

Leola Furman, PhD
Associate Professor
Department of Social Work
University of North Dakota

Spirituality in Social Work: New Directions

Spirituality in Social Work: New Directions has been co-published simultaneously as *Social Thought,* Volume 18, Number 2 1998.

The *Social Thought* Monographs/"Separates"

Spirituality in Social Work: New Directions, edited by Edward R. Canda

Postmodernism, Religion and the Future of Social Work, edited by Roland G. Meinert, John T. Pardeck, and John W. Murphy

Spirituality in social
 work : new directions /

These books were published simultaneously as special thematic issues of the *Social Thought* and are available bound separately. Visit Haworth's website at http://www.haworthpressinc.com to search our online catalog for complete tables of contents and ordering information for these and other publications. Or call 1-800-HAWORTH (outside US/Canada: 607-722-5857), Fax: 1-800-895-0582 (outside US/Canada: 607-771-0012), or e-mail: getinfo@haworthpressinc.com

Spirituality
in Social Work:
New Directions

Edward R. Canda
Editor

Spirituality in Social Work: New Directions has been co-published simultaneously as *Social Thought,* Volume 18, Number 2 1998.

The Haworth Pastoral Press
An Imprint of
The Haworth Press, Inc.
New York • London

Published by

The Haworth Pastoral Press, 10 Alice Street, Binghamton, NY 13904-1580 USA

The Haworth Pastoral Press is an imprint of The Haworth Press, Inc., 10 Alice Street, Binghamton, NY 13904-1580 USA.

Spirituality in Social Work: New Directions has been co-published
simultaneously as *Social Thought,* Volume 18, Number 2 1998.

The development, preparation, and publication of this work has been undertaken with great care.
However, the publisher, employees, editors, and agents of The Haworth Press and all imprints of
The Haworth Press, Inc., including The Haworth Medical Press and The Pharmaceutical Products
Press, are not responsible for any errors contained herein or for consequences that may ensue from
use of materials or information contained in this work. Opinions expressed by the author(s) are not
necessarily those of The Haworth Press, Inc.

Cover design by Thomas J. Mayshock Jr.

Library of Congress Cataloging-in-Publication Data

Canda, Edward R.
    Spirituality in social work : new directions / Edward R. Canda, editor.
      p. cm.
    Includes bibliographical references and index.
    ISBN 0-7890-0515-8 (alk. paper)
    1. Social service–Religious aspects. 2. Spiritual life. 3. Spirituality.
HV530.C36 1998
361.3'2'01–dc21
                                                                     98-17375
                                                                             CIP

INDEXING & ABSTRACTING

Contributions to this publication are selectively indexed or abstracted in print, electronic, online, or CD-ROM version(s) of the reference tools and information services listed below. This list is current as of the copyright date of this publication. See the end of this section for additional notes.

- *Abstracts of Research in Pastoral Care & Counseling,* Loyola College, 7135 Minstrel Way, Suite 101, Columbia, MD 21045
- *Applied Social Sciences Index & Abstracts (ASSIA) (Online: ASSI via Data-Star) (CDRom: ASSIA Plus),* Bowker-Sauer Limited, Maypole House, Maypole Road, East Grinstead, West Sussex, RH191HH, England
- *caredata CD: the social and community care database,* National Institute for Social Work, 5 Tavistock Place, London WC1H 9SS, England
- *CNPIEC Reference Guide: Chinese National Directory of Foreign Periodicals,* P.O. Box 88, Beijing, People's Republic of China
- *IBZ International Bibliography of Periodical Literature,* Zeller Verlag GmbH & Co., P.O.B. 1949, d-49009 Osnabruck, Germany
- *INTERNET ACCESS (& additional networks) Bulletin Board for Libraries ("BUBL") coverage of information resources on INTERNET, JANET, and other networks.*
  - <URL:http://bubl.ac.uk/>
  - The new locations will be found under <URL:http://bubl.ac.uk/link/>.
  - Any existing BUBL users who have problems finding information on the new service should contact the BUBL help line by sending e-mail to <bubl@bubl.ac.uk>.
  The Andersonian Library, Curran Building, 101 St. James Road, Glasgow G4 0NS, Scotland
- *National Periodical Library,* Guide to Social Science & Religion, P. O. Box 3278, Clearwater, FL 33767
- *Orere Source, The (Pastoral Abstracts),* P.O. Box 362, Harbert, MI 49115
- *Peace Research Abstracts Journal,* Peace Research Institute, 25 Dundana Avenue, Dundas, Ontario L9H 4ES, Canada

(continued)

- *Sage Race Relations Abstracts,* University of Manchester, Department of American Studies, Manchester M13 9PL, England

- *Sage Urban Studies Abstracts (SUSA),* Sage Publications, Inc., 2455 Teller Road, Newbury Park, CA 91320

- *Social Work Abstracts,* National Association of Social Workers, 750 First Street NW, 8th Floor, Washington, DC 20002

- *Sociological Abstracts (SA),* Sociological Abstracts, Inc., P.O. Box 22206, San Diego, CA 92192-0206

- *Theology Digest (also made available on CD-ROM),* St. Louis University, 3650 Lindell Boulevard, St. Louis, MO 63108

- *Violence and Abuse Abstracts: A Review of Current Literature on Interpersonal Violence (VAA),* Sage Publications, Inc., 2455 Teller Road, Newbury Park, CA 91320

SPECIAL BIBLIOGRAPHIC NOTES

related to special journal issues (separates)
and indexing/abstracting

❑ indexing/abstracting services in this list will also cover material in any "separate" that is co-published simultaneously with Haworth's special thematic journal issue or DocuSerial. Indexing/abstracting usually covers material at the article/chapter level.

❑ monographic co-editions are intended for either non-subscribers or libraries which intend to purchase a second copy for their circulating collections.

❑ monographic co-editions are reported to all jobbers/wholesalers/approval plans. The source journal is listed as the "series" to assist the prevention of duplicate purchasing in the same manner utilized for books-in-series.

❑ to facilitate user/access services all indexing/abstracting services are encouraged to utilize the co-indexing entry note indicated at the bottom of the first page of each article/chapter/contribution.

❑ this is intended to assist a library user of any reference tool (whether print, electronic, online, or CD-ROM) to locate the monographic version if the library has purchased this version but not a subscription to the source journal.

❑ individual articles/chapters in any Haworth publication are also available through the Haworth Document Delivery Service (HDDS).

Spirituality in Social Work: New Directions

CONTENTS

Preface   ix
Elizabeth D. Smith

Foreword   xi
Edward R. Canda

Social Work's Conceptualization of Spirituality   1
Maria M. Carroll

Spirituality and Religion in Graduate Social Work Education   15
Robin Russel

An Exploration of Intuition for Social Work Practice
and Education   31
Barbara B. Luoma

Taoism and the Strengths Perspective   47
Terry Lea Koenig
Richard N. Spano

Between Two Worlds: The Psychospiritual Crisis
of a Dying Adolescent   67
Barbara Peo Early

The Relation Between Church and State:
Issues in Social Work and the Law   81
Lawrence E. Ressler

Afterword: Linking Spirituality and Social Work:
Five Themes for Innovation   97
Edward R. Canda

Index   107

ABOUT THE EDITOR

Edward R. Canda, PhD, is Associate Professor in the School of Social Welfare at the University of Kansas in Lawrence, Kansas. He has been a Fulbright Scholar and a Korea Foundation Fellow for the study of East Asian philosophy and religion in South Korea. In 1990, Dr. Canda founded the Society for Spirituality and Social Work, for which he now serves on the Board of Directors. He has published more than 30 articles and book chapters on connections between spiritual diversity, culture, and social work. His forthcoming book *Contemporary Human Behavior Theory: A Critical Perspective for Social Work* (co-authored with Susan Robbins, PhD, and Pranab Chatterjee, PhD) integrates content on spirituality, religion, and transpersonal theory throughout each chapter.

Preface

Clearly there is a strong movement afoot among Americans to re-integrate religious ritual and spiritual affirmation back into their daily lives. In some cases this movement takes on the familiar face of the traditional, while for others it finds new expression. The popular media reports that Americans are predominantly theistic, attend religious services regularly, and find spirituality to be very important in their lives. Americans are re-embracing their traditional Judeo-Christian roots. Television is successfully launching prime-time shows with strong Christian content such as *Touched by an Angel* and *Nothing Sacred*. This profile of Americans as believers is not necessarily new, given that the founding fathers (and mothers) of this country placed their trust in God. What is new is the myriad forms of acceptable spiritual expression now embraced by Americans. On the brink of a new millennium and with global telecommunications at their fingertips, ancient wisdom and traditions of the East have been readily adopted by much of the American public. *Time* magazine featured an issue on *America's Fascination with Buddhism* (October, 1997) citing two recently released motion pictures, *Seven Years in Tibet* and *Kundun*, as supporting evidence. Thus, it seems, according to the *New York Times Magazine* (December 7, 1997) special issue *God Decentralized*, that "Americans are still among the most religious people on the planet. But these days, they're busy inventing unorthodox ways to get where they're going." If it is true that the mass media has a finger on the collective pulse of America, then it is clear that whether Christian, Jewish, Buddhist, Muslim or, as one contributor to the issue wrote, "Alone in a lofty place," Americans are expressing their overwhelming interest in spiritual matters.

Social work, with its holistic focus on person-in-environment, has long acknowledged the importance of mind, body, spirit integration. Social workers in hospice and healthcare settings have been among the first in the

---

Elizabeth D. Smith, DSW, is Editor of *Social Thought*.

[Haworth co-indexing entry note]: "Preface." Smith, Elizabeth D., Smith. Co-published simultaneously in *Social Thought* (The Haworth Pastoral Press, an imprint of The Haworth Press, Inc.) Vol. 18, No. 2, 1998, pp. xi-xii; and: *Spirituality in Social Work: New Directions* (ed: Edward R. Canda) The Haworth Pastoral Press, an imprint of The Haworth Press, Inc., 1998, pp. ix-x. Single or multiple copies of this article are available for a fee from The Haworth Document Delivery Service [1-800-342-9678, 9:00 a.m. - 5:00 p.m. (EST). E-mail address: getinfo@haworthpressinc.com].

profession to explore the significance of religious/spiritual belief as a means of relieving psychological distress in the face of life-threatening illness and death. Mental health social workers have been close on their heels with models of practice that include elements of spiritual/religious interventions such as meditation, acknowledging a higher power, spiritual meaning-making, Buddhist ego-disattachment and the existential act of confronting one's mortality. While many of these clinical models have been in use for a number of years, the viability of treating the individual's spiritual health is just recently being openly accepted. Transpersonal experiences such as visions, out-of-body experiences, and psychic phenomena are no longer necessarily viewed as pathological, but are now considered within the realm of possibility and worthy of research. In fact, empirical studies evaluating the efficacy of such experiences, as well as spiritual interventions, are now being funded.

Given this post-modern context for social work practice of multiple spiritual realities, the profession faces a profound clinical challenge. It must assist its clientele in addressing the specific subjectivity of religious/ spiritual values, while remaining value-free and objective. It must develop explanatory and change theories, as well as models of practice, that address the particularity of belief without adopting belief. All of this must be done in the spirit of inclusion and within the context of client self-determination, the hallmark values of social work.

This collection dedicated to Spirituality and Social Work is a landmark volume. It is the first of its kind to bring together the cutting-edge themes of spirituality and social work from the perspective of social work academics and practitioners alike. It offers the reader a glimpse into the future of social work where the spiritual is fully integrated with the physical, psychological, and social aspects of the individual, and worthy of professional attention. The authors that have contributed to this volume are sensitized to the inextricable nature of spirituality as a defining aspect of each individual. In their writings they are attempting to shed light on what social work practice in this realm looks like and what it will mean for the future development of the profession.

As Vice-President of the Society for Spirituality and Social Work, and as Editor of *Social Thought*, I am one of many who are participating in the social work response to the American spiritual/religious movement. This response will take us well into the twenty-first century and define our practice for the new millennium. With the reading of this issue, you may join in that response.

Elizabeth D. Smith

Foreword

It is my pleasure to serve as editor for *Spirituality in Social Work: New Directions*. This volume is very timely because of the rapid increase of interest in the topic of spirituality among social work educators and practitioners discussed by the authors. Many social workers are seeking guidance for how to address the religious and spiritual aspects of people's lives while respecting and appreciating the diverse and sometimes conflicting expressions of spirituality for individuals and communities. In response, the contributors to this collection present an overview of the connection between spirituality and social work, including its current status and possibilities for continuing innovation and exploration.

The authors are all active within the Society for Spirituality and Social Work, which supports the development of approaches to social work practice, theory, research, policy, and education that are respectful of spirituality's diverse religious and nonreligious forms. I founded this society in 1990 and transferred the Society's activity to publish refereed articles on spirituality to *Social Thought* in 1994. Now, under the directorship of Robin Russel, the Society for Spirituality and Social Work is active in producing a newsletter, presenting local and national conferences, networking internationally, and advocating for spiritual awareness in all aspects of the profession.[1] We in the Society would like to give special appreciation and support to *Social Thought* with Joseph Shields as past editor, and Elizabeth Smith as current editor, for its important role in disseminating scholarship on spirituality and social services.

The first two articles give an overview of the current state of connection between spirituality and social work scholarship and education. Maria Carroll presents a critical review of conceptualizations of spirituality in the social work literature and highlights implications for theory and practice. Her article reinforces the important distinction between spirituality as a

---

[Haworth co-indexing entry note]: "Foreword." Canda, Edward R. Co-published simultaneously in *Social Thought* (The Haworth Pastoral Press, an imprint of The Haworth Press, Inc.) Vol. 18, No. 2, 1998, pp. xiii-xv; and: *Spirituality in Social Work: New Directions* (ed: Edward R. Canda) The Haworth Pastoral Press, an imprint of The Haworth Press, Inc., 1998, pp. xi-xiii. Single or multiple copies of this article are available for a fee from The Haworth Document Delivery Service [1-800-342-9678, 9:00 a.m. - 5:00 p.m. (EST). E-mail address: getinfo@haworth.com].

fundamental, universal quality of the human being and its manifestation in religious or nonreligious contexts. She also draws out the significance for human development of integrating spirituality as the essence of human nature together with spirituality as one dimension of human experience. Robin Russel presents an analysis of the way spirituality is presently taught within MSW programs. She documents the rapid increase of specialized courses on this topic, reflecting recent attention given to religious and spiritual diversity in the Council on Social Work Education's Curriculum Policy Statement as well as general trends in our society and profession.

The next two articles present innovations in social work practice and education that draw on previously neglected resources for personal and professional spiritual insight. Barbara Luoma advocates for the inclusion of training that can enhance the intuition of social workers. She points out that practitioners have long recognized practice wisdom and intuition as critical ingredients in successful helping, but that related skills have rarely been addressed in coursework or training programs. A study of students in her own courses demonstrates their strong interest in this topic and the need to address it in education. Terry Koenig and Rick Spano explore insights from Taoism for enhancing a strengths perspective on social work practice. Taoism is an ancient Chinese spiritual tradition that honors intuition and spontaneous creativity and guides us to move beyond dichotomous thinking and alienated ways of relating to the world.

Barbara Early presents a clinical application of the Transegoic model with a dying adolescent. In her in-depth case study, she addresses her young client's psychospiritual issues through his dream images. Next, Lawrence Ressler directs our attention to the importance of spirituality for macro level social work practice and policy development. He discusses the historical and continuing tensions between church and state that impact social services delivered through sectarian religious auspices. His article illuminates the special dilemmas that arise when spiritual beliefs and practices related to helping are linked to religious institutions and community support systems. In the final article, I provide suggestions for future efforts to link spirituality to social work by drawing on the issues and recommendations raised by the previous authors.

The Society for Spirituality and Social Work has sponsored three national conferences (1995, 1996 and 1997), the themes of which summarize well the status of connection between spirituality and social work. The first conference theme was "Retrieving the Soul of Social Work," emphasizing the profession's recovery of its heritage of spiritual perspectives and commitments beginning in the mid-1980s. The second conference theme was "Expressing the Soul of Social Work," celebrating the current innovations arising from the rapprochement with spirituality. The theme of the third conference was "Nurturing the Soul of Social Work," focused on the Society's commitment to support practitioners and scholars in social service that honors and encourages spiritual development and justice for all people of diverse religious and non-religious paths. It is my hope that this volume spreads word of these developments and encourages creative and soulful cooperation among social workers of all spiritual perspectives.

Edward R. Canda

NOTE

1. For more information on the Society for Spirituality and Social Work, please write to: Robin Russel, PhD, Director, Society for Spirituality and Social Work, School of Social Work, University of Nebraska at Omaha, Omaha, NE 68182-0293.

Social Work's Conceptualization of Spirituality

Maria M. Carroll

SUMMARY. The social work literature reflects an increasing interest in spirituality; however, social workers appear to have different meanings of the term spirituality. Building on Canda's (1988a) conceptualization of spirituality, this article identifies and defines two meanings: spirituality-as-essence of human nature and spirituality-as-one-dimension of human experience. The different meanings of these concepts have important theoretical and practice implications. The theoretical implications include spirituality and the person as well as the beginning and development of a person's spirituality. The practice implications include views of well-being, dysfunctional behavior, and approaches to treatment. This article clarifies these definitions and their implications in order to promote greater conceptual consistency within the social work profession. *[Article copies available for a fee from The Haworth Document Delivery Service: 1-800-342-9678. E-mail address: getinfo@haworthpressinc.com]*

A resurgence is underway in the social work profession's interest in spirituality. This resurgence is reflected in recent presentations and publications on this topic (Carroll, 1990; Cornett, 1992; Cowley, 1993; Cowley & Derezotes, 1994; Logan, 1990; Sermabeikian, 1994; Sheridan, Bullis, Adcock, Berlin, & Miller, 1992; Titone, 1991). However, there are various conceptualizations of spirituality and the term is not used consistently.

Maria M. Carroll, PhD, is Associate Professor, Department of Social Work, Delaware State University, Dover, DE 19904.

[Haworth co-indexing entry note]: "Social Work's Conceptualization of Spirituality." Carroll, Maria M. Co-published simultaneously in *Social Thought* (The Haworth Pastoral Press, an imprint of The Haworth Press, Inc.) Vol. 18, No. 2, 1998, pp. 1-13; and: *Spirituality in Social Work: New Directions* (ed: Edward R. Canda) The Haworth Pastoral Press, an imprint of The Haworth Press, Inc., 1998, pp. 1-13. Single or multiple copies of this article are available for a fee from The Haworth Document Delivery Service [1-800-342-9678, 9:00 a.m. - 5:00 p.m. (EST). E-mail address: getinfo@haworthpressinc.com].

The current social work literature does not always address variations in meanings of this important component of human experience. In order to promote greater clarity and consistency in professional discourse, this article seeks to refine the conceptualization of spirituality. First, the concepts of religion and spirituality are distinguished. Then, two aspects of spirituality are examined in more detail, based on a review of the literature. Finally, both the theoretical and practice implications of the two aspects of spirituality are discussed.

SPIRITUALITY AND RELIGION

A clear conceptualization of spirituality can begin with its differentiation from religion. Canda and Joseph recognized the importance of such a distinction between religion and spirituality (Sanzenbach, Canda, & Joseph, 1989). Several authors (Dudley & Helfgott, 1990; Ortiz, 1991; Titone, 1991) distinguish between the two concepts as follows: spirituality refers to one's basic nature and the process of finding meaning and purpose whereas religion involves a set of organized, institutionalized beliefs and social functions as a means of spiritual expression and experience. Many people think of spirituality as basically personal and religion as inherently social. For some individuals, spirituality and religion are inextricably linked; for others, the two are distinct. This discussion will focus on spirituality as a general aspect of human nature and development rather than particular religious beliefs and institutions.

SPIRITUALITY: ESSENCE AND DIMENSION

Edward Canda has explored spirituality and social work extensively. In developing a conceptualization of spirituality, Canda (1988a) invited others to participate in a scholarly dialogue to clarify and elaborate on the conceptualization.

Canda (1986, 1988a) interviewed 18 social workers who had either written or presented papers on spirituality regarding their insights "with explicit consideration of the holistic person-in-environment orientation of social work and in relation to the connection between knowledge, values, and skills in social work" (1988a, p. 31). The perspectives Canda elicited from his interviewees included atheism, theistic humanism, and five religious perspectives (Christianity, Judaism, Buddhism, Shamanism, and existentialism). These perspectives on spirituality shared in common seven recurrent themes: spirituality (1) "is an intrinsic and irreducible aspect of the person" (Canda, 1988a, p. 41); (2) is expressed through individual development and relationship with the environment; (3) integrates all aspects of the person; (4) involves the search for meaning and purpose; (5) involves loving relationship with all which exists; (6) provides a way of understanding human suffering and alienation; and (7) integrates the everyday worldly aspects with the transcendent aspects.

From his exploratory research as well as his literature review, Canda (1988a) conceptualized spirituality as

> the gestalt of the total process of human life and development, encompassing the biological, mental, social, and spiritual aspects . . . a quality of sacredness and meaningfulness in self, other people, the nonhuman world, and the ground of being (as conceived in theistic, nontheistic, or atheistic terms) . . . associated with a dimension of reality that exceeds the ordinary limits of human understanding and description. (pp. 41, 43)

In later discussing this conceptualization, Canda (1990) refers to spirituality as the wholeness of humanity and not to any one component (biological, mental, social, or spiritual). He also defines spirituality in a narrower sense, a component of one's experience, which is "the person's search for a sense of meaning and morally fulfilling relationships between oneself, other people, the encompassing universe, and the ontological ground of existence" (p. 13). These two meanings, the wholeness of humanity and one component, will be identified here as *spirituality-as-essence* and *spirituality-as-one-dimension*. The presence of dual meanings in the concept of spirituality does not necessarily say that these meanings are dichotomous. The term spirituality is also used to include both of the meanings (Canda, 1988a; Siporin, 1985). The multiple meanings of the concept of spirituality are recurrent in the social work literature.

Descriptions of spirituality-as-essence (originating from the deepest core of the person or having to do with fundamental human nature) have included the human spirit as "the principle of life and vital energy" (Corbett, 1925, p. 225), a supernatural essence which is the source of the soul's internal resources (Siporin, 1985), "the ground of our being" (Joseph, 1988, p. 444), and a natural order which underlies spirituality (Constable, 1990). Sermabeikian (1994) referred to Jung's efforts to prove that spirituality is "the essence of human nature" (p. 179) through his work in depth psychology and comparative mythology. Keith-Lucas (1960) referred to the necessity to learn more about human nature. Imre (1971) and others (Bradford, 1969; Krill, 1966, 1969; Rubin, 1962; Stretch, 1967; Turner,

1968; Weick, 1983, 1987) referred to a potential and capacity for growth and change. For Weick (1983), the capacity for self-transformation involves an inner sense of knowing or wisdom and is an internal response to opportunities for healthy development. This capacity leads to her advocacy for a new social work paradigm which is based not on disease but on health. Although Weick (1983) does not use the term spirituality, her emphasis on self-healing resources is very similar to others' descriptions of spirituality-as-essence. Each of these descriptions either states or implies a built-in nature or essence which provides the motivating energy toward meeting the potential for self-development and self-transformation.

Social workers have also viewed spirituality as a *part* of human existence, experience, and behavior. For instance, according to Hughes (1984), human beings have a built-in nature to fulfill which includes a spiritual *aspect*. Canda (1986, 1988a, 1990) has stated that spirituality is an intrinsic and irreducible *aspect* of the person. Siporin (1986) claimed that social work theory neglected the person's spiritual *side* by emphasizing self-fulfillment and self-realization on a personal or ego level (rather than a transpersonal level). Bullis (1996) defined spirituality "as the relationship of the human person to something or someone who transcends themselves" (p. 2) thus emphasizing the part of the person which relates with the transcendent. Cornett (1992) has proposed that social work expand its perspective from bio-psycho-social to a bio-psycho-social-spiritual model thus making spiritual issues a "legitimate clinical focus and provide for a more complete understanding of clients' strengths, weaknesses, and problems" (p. 102). Cowley (1993) pointed out that traditional models (reductionistic, behavioral, linear, quantitative) are insufficient to address current problems such as nuclear weapons, AIDS, homelessness, holes in the ozone layer, ecological pollution, violence, and love hunger so that spiritual approaches are necessary. These authors state or imply that spirituality is one *part* or *aspect* of oneself. According to Canda (1990), this spiritual aspect relates to the search for a sense of meaning, fulfillment, and moral standards for relating with oneself, the environment, and the ground of being, however people understand it.

In summary, the view of spirituality-as-essence refers to a core nature which provides a sense of personal wholeness and an energy that motivates people to actualize their potential for self-development and self-transformation. The view of spirituality-as-one-dimension, however, refers specifically to behaviors and experiences involved in developing meaning and a relationship with God, the transcendent, or ultimate reality. Spirituality-as-essence provides the context and direction for spirituality-as-one-dimension. In addition, both meanings may be included in an overall concept of spirituality. When the distinction between spirituality-as-essence and spirituality-as-one-dimension is kept in mind, some clarity is achieved about what the various social work authors mean when they refer to the spiritual. The difference in the two meanings–essence and dimension–generates theoretical questions such as: (1) how is a person's spirituality related to the various parts–the biological, psychological (emotional and mental), and social; and (2) when does spirituality start, and how does it develop?

THEORETICAL IMPLICATIONS

Spirituality and the Person

Spirituality has been described as relationship or interconnectedness with self, others and God–with all that exists in the universe (Canda, 1983; Constable, 1990). From the view of spirituality-as-essence, spirituality might be described both as a state of interconnectedness with existence *and* as the energy which works toward this interconnectedness.

When spirituality is one dimension equal with the other dimensions (biological, psychological, and social), it apparently refers only to the relationship with God (or a trans-personal reality–a reality beyond the self) or to the search for that relationship. This relationship has also been discussed as relationship with a transcendent and unconditionally loving, ultimate source of reality or creation (Imre, 1971), and "with ultimate sources in inspiration, energy, and motivation" (Titone, 1991, p. 8). Spirituality "seeks union with the universe. The spiritual dimension seeks to transcend self and relate the individual to the ultimate" (Joseph, 1988, p. 444). The spiritual dimension involves a "search for transcendent values, meaning, experience, and development; for knowledge of an ultimate reality; for a belonging and relatedness with the moral universe and community; and for union with the immanent, supernatural powers that guide people and the universe for good or evil" (Siporin, 1985, p. 210). These descriptions indicate that the spiritual-as-dimension concerns the relationship with God or the transcendent (or however the transcendent is conceptualized).

One way in which the spiritual-as-dimension is manifest is in the caring and commitment which people have toward each other. In this sense, spirituality, as one dimension (namely, the relationship with God or the transcendent) is reflected in the extent and quality of interconnectedness between self and others; the interconnectedness itself is spirituality-as-essence.

Beginning and Growth of Spirituality

When is spirituality considered to begin in one's life? Is spirituality always present even at birth or does it appear later in life when the person begins to relate consciously with the transcendent or even later when commitment to a relationship with the transcendent and to "spiritual" values are a conscious choice? And once begun, how does spirituality grow?

Some social workers consider spirituality as essence, and, therefore, it is always present. The growth of spirituality-as-essence occurs through a developmental process. The goal of this process is fulfillment of one's potential which is also called individuation, self-actualization, and self-realization. When attempting to define casework with a one word description, Richmond (1930) used the word 'individuation' which reflects the process of developing individuality and does not imply "that there is necessarily a wrong to be righted or a disease to be eradicated" (p. 477). The concept of individuation is also consistent with Jungian psychology, which offers a broad theory of human behavior and development through the concepts of the collective unconscious and the Self archetype as well as a teleologic approach to personality development (Borenzweig, 1984). Richmond (1930) quoted from Jung,

> A person is only half understood when one knows how everything in him came about. Only a dead man can be explained in terms of the past, a living one must be otherwise explained. Life is not made up of yesterdays only, nor is it understood and explained by reducing today to yesterday. Life has also a tomorrow, and today is only understood if we are able to add the indications of tomorrow to our knowledge of what was yesterday. (p. 485)

Her quote suggests her seeing hope and possibilities in one's potential very similar to the beliefs of Jung as well as to others who subsequently have described spirituality as the essence of human nature.

More specifically, Joseph (1987) explored religious and spiritual issues throughout the developmental life-cycle by drawing on the works of Fowler (1981). Similarly, Kilpatrick and Holland (1990) suggested that stages of faith development parallel psycho-social developmental stages. The existentialists referred to a striving for self-actualization (Bradford, 1969; Imre, 1971; Krill, 1966, 1969; Rubin, 1962; Stretch, 1967; Turner, 1968). Cowley (1993) discussed transpersonal theory described by Wilber, Engler, and Brown (1986) who integrate Western psychologies and Eastern contemplative psychologies to go beyond ego and self-actualization to self-transcendence. Consistent with Richmond, these ideas helped to move the social work emphasis from addressing problems and symptoms to facilitating people's development toward completion or wholeness.

These descriptions of spirituality refer to an essence which always exists regardless of the person's conscious awareness of it. Spiritual growth would reflect *qualitative* changes in one's view of the world which leads to greater connectedness with self, others, and all existence.

From the view of spirituality-as-one-dimension, spirituality would become evident when the person begins to have a conscious relationship with the transcendent. Spiritual growth, then, would be *quantitative* in terms of a greater and deeper relationship with the transcendent.

Several authors (Dudley & Helfgott, 1990; Hess, 1980; Joseph, 1988; Ortiz, 1991; Siporin, 1985; Titone, 1991) have viewed spirituality as the human search for meaning in life or a purpose of life. How this search is understood depends on which concept of spirituality is being considered or addressed. For instance, in discussing spirituality-as-one-dimension, Canda (1988a) described the search for meaning in life as arising from an innate need which involves satisfying prior developmental needs (e.g., material requirements, loving social relationships) in the process of self-realization. Thus, from this perspective the need (for meaning of life) seems to be dependent on *first* satisfying the more basic developmental needs and then moving on to search for meaning in life through a quantitatively greater relationship with God or the transcendent. From the spirituality-as-essence view, the need is at least partially met in the very *process* of satisfying the basic developmental needs. Spiritual growth is reflected in qualitative changes in how one makes sense of the meaning of life which, Sermabeikian (1994) notes, is a necessary part of the struggle toward human development. The concept of spirituality which includes both meanings suggests both qualitative and quantitative changes in an integrated and ongoing process of meeting basic developmental needs and increasing or deepening one's relationships with the transcendent.

A theme inherent in either view is wholeness; however, the nature of the wholeness is different. When spirituality is regarded as one dimension equal with other dimensions, wholeness refers to the development of consciousness of one's relationship with God or the transcendent. When spirituality is regarded as the essence of human nature and grows through a developmental process or as a combination of essence and dimension, wholeness refers to completion of this process which is conscious connectedness with self, others, and God or the transcendent.

IMPLICATIONS FOR PRACTICE

Regardless of which view (spirituality-as-essence or spirituality-as-one-dimension) is taken, the treatment goal of reducing dysfunctioning and enhancing maximum functioning occurs as people become connected with self, others, and God or the transcendent. The particular view, however, does impact on how the social worker and client view dysfunctioning and treatment.

Spirituality-as-Essence

With the view of spirituality-as-essence, the potential for complete conscious connectedness always exists. The process and goal of becoming consciously connected is to experience and realize one's self which Jung (1928/1966) also calls "the God within" (p. 238). This process implies that lack of consciousness of the connectedness is present in early life, and emergence of that consciousness is part of a healthy developmental process. For those who support spirituality-as-essence, the energy of the spirit—"the principle of life and vital energy" (Corbett, 1925, p. 225)—motivates the person toward conscious connectedness with self, others, and God or the transcendent.

The non-emergence or loss of conscious connectedness is reflected in dysfunctional behaviors and disease. Lack of conscious connectedness or loss of meaning may precipitate a crisis. In the Chinese language, the character depicting 'crisis' means both danger and opportunity. When the behaviors are considered to be dangerous, they are typically seen in a totally negative light. When, however, the behavior or crisis is viewed as an opportunity for growth, then a new and positive view emerges that potentially places the crisis in a different perspective which is characteristic of the next stage of spiritual development. As an opportunity, disruption of the bio-psycho-social status quo opens a door to a way through which one's potential may emerge. This view is reflected in some recovering alcoholics gratefully remarking that without the alcoholism, "I wouldn't be where I am today." Turning a major difficulty into an opportunity for growth allows one's potential to be expressed. In other words, dysfunction or disease may be part of a process. In this sense, mental and psychosocial disorders and their symptoms (alcoholism, depression, work inhibition, impulsivity, etc.) can be understood as a part of an overall developmental process which involves accepting and reframing the crisis thereby transforming it into a growth opportunity.

Social work treatment includes both the social worker-client relationship and specific modalities or tools. The social worker's authenticity or conscious connectedness with himself or herself establishes the foundation for a relationship which involves his or her honoring the client's innate wisdom about his or her own life, respecting the client's right to determine meaning of the events of his or her life, sharing with the client through the relationship the belief in the client's strength and power (Weick, 1983b), and empowering the client by helping him or her to realize and use what he or she already has (Rappaport, 1985; Sermabeikian, 1994; Weick, 1983b). This two-step process involves the clinician fully accepting the client where he or she is and thereby providing space and structure within which the client taps into his or her inner power, gains self-trust, and finds freedom for self-discovery.

A number of tools have been linked with spirituality and spiritual growth. These tools include prayer, meditation (Canda, 1983; Keefe, 1976, 1986; Sheridan et al., 1992), contemplation, ritual, scripture study, use of the natural environment as a healing context (Canda, 1983) and work with a wide range of consciousness states (Canda, 1988b) including dreams and imagery. The therapeutic tools help to establish an environment within which the client can accomplish what he or she wants as well as to facilitate the developmental process of the client's moving toward connecting with all which exists—with self, others, and God or the transcendent. The outside forces (i.e., the dynamics in the relationship, ritual, physical setting) mobilize the internal healing forces which bring about a positive change (Weick, 1983b).

Spirituality-as-One-Dimension

With the view of spirituality-as-one-dimension, spiritual issues are only those which address a person's conscious search for meaning and a relationship with God or the transcendent. If the social worker's focus is primarily on psycho-social issues, he or she may not recognize spiritual issues at all, yet spiritual issues may be central to the client's crisis. If and when the social worker does recognize such issues, he or she may think they are not appropriate to address, may not know how to handle them, or may not see their relevance. Thus important issues and resources may be missed.

This gap may lead the social worker to see psycho-social dysfunction primarily in terms of negative behaviors. The crisis raised by these behaviors is then seen as being dangerous, having no redeeming value, and needing to be directly eradicated. Such a view of dysfunctioning does not include spiritual (-as-one-dimension) issues or consider the interrelationship among the biological, psychological, social, and spiritual (-as-one-dimension and -as-essence) issues.

With the view of spirituality-as-one-dimension, many of the tools previously discussed may be used. These tools, however, will be used *only* in order to increase one's conscious search for meaning and connectedness and relatedness with the transcendent, which is expressed explicitly through the person's beliefs and behaviors.

Integration of Essence and Dimension of Spirituality in Practice

In practice, these two views of spirituality are not necessarily mutually exclusive. Indeed, Canda's writings have emphasized that spirituality-as-essence and -as-dimension are inter-related and complementary. The view that one's spirituality(-as-essence) always exists requires that social workers value the full breadth of the individual's resources and be aware that all these resources exist even prior to a time when the person makes a conscious decision to choose a relationship with God or the transcendent.

Clinical approaches incorporating both views, spirituality-as-essence and spirituality-as-one-dimension, can be instrumental in reducing suffering and enhancing psycho-social functioning. The two views may be combined in various ways.

The first approach or way addresses dysfunctioning and suffering which frequently arise from blocked growth due to difficult life events. Building on the view of spirituality-as-essence, the social worker would help the client to consider these events differently by tapping into and trusting one's inner wisdom in order to gain a new understanding about how the socialization process has blocked growth (Weick, 1987) and to discover new meanings so that the difficulty is transformed into a growth opportunity and becomes accepted as part of one's whole life. In this way, the suffering is reduced and functioning is improved. From the perspective of spirituality-as-one-dimension, the social worker would draw on the person's beliefs and behaviors which directly reflect his or her belief systems and sense of relatedness with the transcendent. These beliefs and behaviors may be used as supportive resources or strengths in facing and overcoming problems (Canda, 1983, 1988b; Cornett, 1992; Reynolds, 1991; Siporin, 1986; Spencer, 1957) as well as healing (Kilpatrick & Holland, 1990; Sermabeikian, 1994; Siporin, 1986).

A second way to address suffering is through the use of values which provide both meaning and direction and which strongly influence how one handles problems and makes choices and commitments (Kilpatrick & Holland, 1990). Sermabeikian (1994) refers to Jung's belief in using "spiritual" values to help people address difficult issues and change their attitudes (although here again the meaning of the word 'spiritual' is unclear).

A third way is through the use of intervention tools (meditation, imagery, etc.) which access realms beyond the personal *and* facilitate healing of unresolved personal issues, in some cases almost simultaneously. For instance, tools which assist looking within the self as well as connecting with the universe may seem unrelated to the early work of recovery from chemical addiction. However, clients report seeing the relationship in many ways which include experiencing powerlessness, releasing negative feelings and pent-up emotional energy, reframing past experiences, and expanding one's vision of reality. In addition, clients have found these tools helpful in their 12-step work. For instance, a different and broader perspective facilitates identifying and beginning to accept one's weaknesses, faults, and strengths which is integral to a fourth step inventory. The fear of acknowledging one's faults to another person (the fifth step) or of making amends to a person for wrongs done (the ninth step) may be eased by increasing courage and strength with the experiential realization of one's worth as a person as well as the interconnectedness among people (Carroll, 1993). Canda (1988b) noted that social work needs to develop guidelines for assessing client willingness and readiness to use these transpersonal forces and tools. In addition, the clinician needs to develop the art and skills required for providing these tools and, when necessary, to make appropriate referrals.

CONCLUSIONS

To clarify social work's conceptualization of spirituality, two different meanings of spirituality have been identified; these are spirituality-as-essence and spirituality-as-one-dimension. The view of spirituality-as-essence refers to a core nature which provides the motivating energy toward meeting the potential for self-development and self-transformation. The view of spirituality-as-one-dimension refers specifically to one's search for meaning and relationship with God, the transcendent, or ultimate reality.

This author contends that the meaning of spirituality is best conceptualized as both the essence and a key dimension of human nature. Spirituality in some form is a developing essence in the people's lives, and—for many—an important dimension as well. When social workers partialize or deny the spirituality (either as-essence or as-one-dimension) of their clients, the fulfillment of people's potential for wholeness and creative transformation is restricted. Spirituality is not the exclusive isolated domain of the ministerial professions. Since social workers generally strive toward a holistic understanding of the person-in-environment, social workers need to address spirituality. However, to address the spirituality of our clients is not to practice religion but is to affirm the wholeness of their being.

REFERENCES

Borenzweig, H. (1984). *Jung and social work.* New York: University Press of America.

Bradford, K. (1969). *Existentialism and casework.* New York: Jason Aronson.

Bullis, R. K. (1996). *Spirituality in social work practice.* Washington, DC: Taylor & Francis.

Canda, E. R. (1983). General implications of shamanism for clinical social work. *International Social Work, 26*(4), 14-22.

Canda, E. R. (1986). *A conceptualization of spirituality for social work: Its issues and implications.* Unpublished doctoral dissertation, Ohio State University, Columbus.

Canda, E. R. (1988a). Conceptualizing spirituality for social work: Insights from diverse perspectives. *Social Thought, 14*(1), 30-46.

Canda, E. R. (1988b). Spirituality, religious diversity, and social work practice. *Social Casework, 69*(4), 238-247.

Canda, E. R. (1990). Afterword: Spirituality reexamined. *Spirituality and Social Work Communicator, 1*(1), 13-14.

Carroll, M. M. (1990). Paper presented at the International Transpersonal Conference, Eugene, Oregon.

Carroll, M. M. (1993). *Spiritual growth of recovering alcoholic adult children of alcoholics.* Unpublished doctoral dissertation. University of Maryland at Baltimore (University Microfilms International No. 9319831).

Constable, R. (1990). Spirituality and social work: Issues to be addressed. *Spirituality and Social Work Communicator, 1*(1), 4-6.

Corbett, L. (1925). Spiritual factors in casework. *The Family, VI*(8), 223-227.

Cornett, C. (1992). Toward a more comprehensive personology: Integrating a spiritual perspective into social work practice. *Social Work, 37*(2), 101-2.

Cowley, A. W. (1993). Transpersonal social work: A theory for the 1990s. *Social Work, 38*(5), 527-534.

Cowley, A. S. & Derezotes, D. (1994). Transpersonal psychology and social work education. *Journal of Social Work Education, 30*(1), 32-41.

Dudley, J. R. & Helfgott, C. (1990). Exploring a place for spirituality in the social work curriculum. *Journal of Social Work Education, 26*(3), 287-294.

Fowler, J. (1981). *Stages of faith.* New York: Harper & Row.

Hess, J. J. (1980). Social work's identity crisis: A Christian anthropological response. *Social Thought, 6*(1), 59-69.

Imre, R. W. (1971). A theological view of social casework. *Social Casework, 52*(9), 578-585.

Joseph, M. V. (1988). Religion and social work practice. *Social Casework, 69*(7). 443-452.

Jung, C. G. (1928/1966). The relations Between the ego and the unconscious. In *Collected works (Vol. VII).* (pp. 121-241). Princeton, NJ: Princeton University Press.

Keefe, T. (1975). Meditation and the psychotherapist. *American Journal of Orthopsychiatry, 45*(3), 184-189.

Keefe, T. (1986). Meditation and social work treatment. In F. J. Turner (Ed.).

Social work treatment: interlocking theoretical perspectives (3rd ed.). (pp. 155-180). New York: Free Press.

Kilpatrick, A. C., & Holland, T. P. (1990). The spiritual dimensions of practice. *The Clinical Supervisor, 8*(2), 125-140.

Krill, D. F. (1966). Existentialism: A philosophy for our current revolutions. *Social Service Review, 40*(3), 289-301.

Krill, D. F. (1969). Existential psychotherapy and the problem of anomie. *Social Work, 14*(3), 289-301.

Logan, S. L. (1990). Critical issues in operationalizing the spiritual dimension of social work practice. *Spirituality and Social Work Communicator, 1*(1), 7-9.

Ortiz, L. P. A. (1991). Religious issues: The missing link in social work education. *Spirituality and Social Work Communicator, 2*(2), 13-18.

Rappaport, J. (1985). The power of empowerment language. *Social Policy, 16*(2), 15-21.

Reynolds, B. C. (1991). *An uncharted journey.* Silver Spring, MD: NASW Press.

Richmond, M. (1922). *What is social casework?* New York: Russell Sage Foundation.

Richmond, M. (1930). *The long view.* New York: Russell Sage Foundation.

Rubin, G. K. (1962). Helping a clinic patient modify self-destructive thinking. *Social Work, 7*(1), 76-80.

Sanzenbach, P., Canda, E. R. & Joseph, M. V. (1989). Religion and social work: It's not that simple! *Social Casework, 70*(9), 571-5.

Sermabeikian, P. (1994). Our clients, ourselves: The spiritual perspective and social work practice. *Social Work, 39*(2), 178-183.

Sheridan, M., Bullis, R. K., Adcock, C.R., Berlin, S. D., & Miller, P. C. (1992). Practitioners' personal and professional attitudes and behaviors toward religion and spirituality: Issues for education and practice. *Journal of Social Work Education, 28*(2), 190-203.

Siporin, M. (1983). The therapeutic process in clinical social work. *Social Work, 28*(3), 193-198.

Siporin, M. (1985). Current social work perspectives on clinical practice. *Clinical Social Work Journal, 13*(3), 198-217.

Spencer, S. (1957). Religious and spiritual values in social work practice. *Social Casework, 38*, 519-526.

Stretch, J. J. (1967). Existentialism: A proposed philosophical orientation for social work. *Social Work, 12*(4), 97-102.

Titone, A. M. (1991). Spirituality and psychotherapy in social work practice. *Spirituality and Social Work Communicator, 2*(1), 7-9.

Turner, F. J. (Ed.). (1968). *Differential diagnosis and treatment in social work.* New York: Free Press.

Weick, A. (1983b). Issues in overturning a medical model of social work practice. *Social Work, 28*(6), 467-471.

Weick, A. (1987). Reconceptualizing the philosophical perspective of social work. *Social Service Review, 61*(2), 218-230.

Wilber, K., Engler, J., & Brown, D. (1986). *Transformations of consciousness.* Boston: Shambala Publications.

Spirituality and Religion in Graduate Social Work Education

Robin Russel

SUMMARY. Recognition is growing of the relevance of spirituality to social work practice, which has led to recommendations that spiritual and religious content be included in the M.S.W. curriculum. This article will review the literature on religious and spiritual content in social work education, report the results of a study of the development of spirituality-related courses in M.S.W. programs, and discuss the implications of this research for curriculum development. *[Article copies available for a fee from The Haworth Document Delivery Service: 1-800-342-9678. E-mail address: getinfo@haworthpressinc.com]*

Imagine this situation: You enter a room where adult students are sitting on the floor with crayons drawing pictures of their spiritual paths . . . or debating the relevance and power of prayer . . . or sitting with their eyes closed listening to their teacher drum for them . . . or actively discussing the differences between mystical experiences and psychoses . . . or participating in circle dances from early feminist spiritual traditions. You might wonder where you are. You may well have walked into a meeting of an M.S.W. course on spirituality and social work. While each of the experiences described above may not be typical of most graduate courses on spirituality and social work, clearly these and similar aspects of practice are being explored that have long been neglected in social work education.

Robin Russel, PhD, is Director, Society for Spirituality and Social Work, School of Social Work, University of Nebraska at Omaha, Omaha, NE 68182-0293. Dr. Russel would like to acknowledge and thank Sandi Herzog, MSW, for her assistance with the data collection in this research project while a student at the School of Social Work at the University of Nebraska at Omaha.

[Haworth co-indexing entry note]: "Spirituality and Religion in Graduate Social Work Education." Russel, Robin. Co-published simultaneously in *Social Thought* (The Haworth Pastoral Press, an imprint of The Haworth Press, Inc.) Vol. 18, No. 2, 1998, pp. 15-29; and: *Spirituality in Social Work: New Directions* (ed: Edward R. Canda) The Haworth Pastoral Press, an imprint of The Haworth Press, Inc., 1998, pp. 15-29. Single or multiple copies of this article are available for a fee from The Haworth Document Delivery Service [1-800-342-9678, 9:00 a.m. - 5:00 p.m. (EST). E-mail address: getinfo@ haworthpressinc.com].

The relevance of spirituality and religion to social work practice is increasingly being recognized within the profession. This has led to recommendations that spiritual and religious content be included in the M.S.W. curricula. This article reviews the literature on religious and spiritual content in social work education, reports the results of a study of the development of spirituality courses in M.S.W. programs, and discusses the implications of this research for curriculum development.

REVIEW OF THE LITERATURE

Social work's earliest roots in this country were religious (Leiby, 1985). Religious institutions were the first sponsors of social service programs, and most of the earliest social workers in both the Charity Organization Society and settlement house movements shared a sense of spiritual mission (Holland, 1989; Loewenberg, 1988; Marty, 1980; Netting, Thibault & Ellor, 1990; Siporin, 1986).

Therefore it is not surprising that exploration of religious and spiritual issues had a place in early social work education. The first Council on Social Work Education (C.S.W.E.) Curriculum Policy Statement, used as a standard in the accreditation process, stated that normal "physical, mental, and emotional growth should be considered with due regard to social, cultural, and spiritual influences upon the development of the individual" (Council on Social Work Education, 1953, Section 3543). Spencer (1961) reported the history behind this policy.

> The question of whether or not religious content should be incorporated in social work education received official consideration when the 1952 Curriculum Policy Statement was adopted by the American Association of Schools of Social Work. At the 1952 AASSW business session, concern was expressed because the proposed policy statement made no specific reference to the spiritual aspect of human life. There was strong sentiment that the term "social" was sufficiently inclusive to cover the religious area. Following this discussion, however, the word "spiritual" was inserted in the section on human growth and behavior. (pp. 161-162)

C.S.W.E.'s 1962 Official Statement of Curriculum Policy also included language about the need to study "spiritual" influences to understand the whole person. References to spirituality or religion, however, were not included in either the 1970 or 1984 Curriculum Policy Statements (Marshall, 1991). This change in policy statements reflects a broader change in the profession.

Since the end of the nineteenth century the profession gradually went through interrelated processes of secularization and professionalization (Loewenberg, 1988; Marty, 1980). This included the emulation of psychiatry and its medical model (Holland, 1989) and the embracing of a scientific world view (Faver, 1986; Kilpatrick & Holland, 1990). Empiricism, secular humanism and libertarian morality replaced religion and spirituality as the leading professional sources of ethics and values (Imre, 1984; Siporin, 1982, 1986). Religion and spirituality were increasingly viewed, at best, as unnecessary and irrelevant, and, at worst, as illogical and pathological (Spencer, 1961).

Even though spirituality was mentioned in the 1953 and 1962 Curriculum Policy Statements, there is evidence that by that time interest in the spiritual dimensions of social work practice was already waning both within the profession and in schools of social work (Marty, 1980; Spencer, 1956, 1961). Many commentators have described the lack of interest in religion or spirituality that continued well into the 1980s, on the part of the profession and social work educators (Joseph, 1988; Marty, 1980; Spencer, 1961). The social work literature rarely included treatment of these issues (Joseph, 1987; Marty, 1980; Spencer, 1961).

A resurgence of interest in the interface of spirituality, religion, and social work has occurred in the past decade. This is reflected in the professional literature, presentations at professional conferences, and professional meetings devoted specifically to this topic (Canda, 1995; Joseph, 1987). The social work literature generally distinguishes between the concepts of spirituality and religion. Spirituality is usually defined as an individual search for meaning, purpose and values, while religion is viewed as the institutional context of spiritual beliefs, a social process having to do with shared rituals, beliefs and practice (Canda, 1989; Joseph, 1987; Siporin, 1985).

The renewed professional enthusiasm for religious and spiritual issues has paralleled a resurgence of public interest in spirituality and religion (Canda, 1989; Sheridan, Bullis, Adcock, Berlin & Miller, 1992; Siporin, 1985, 1986). Sociologists of religion have noted the increased interest of the "baby boom" generation (persons born between 1946 and 1964) in spiritual and religious matters and "an openness to new spiritual sensitivities" (Roof, 1993, p. 6).

> Religious and spiritual themes are surfacing in a rich variety of ways–in Eastern religions, in evangelical and fundamentalist teachings, in mysticism and New Age movements, in Goddess worship and other ancient religious rituals, in the mainline churches and synagogues, in Twelve-Step recovery groups, in concern about the

environment, in holistic health, and in personal and social transformation. (Roof, pp. 4-5)

The professional literature on the interface of spirituality, religion, and social work has grown in the last ten years. Numerous authors have addressed the need for social workers to be educated about religious and spiritual issues that impact their practice (e.g., Cowley & Derezotes, 1994; Denton, 1990; Dudley & Helfgott, 1990; Joseph, 1988; Kilpatrick & Holland, 1990; Sermabeikian, 1994; Sheridan et al., 1992).

A number of reasons have been given for the need to include the spiritual and religious dimensions of practice in social work education. Clients express interest in spiritual and religious issues and often identify spiritual problems or goals (Dudley & Helfgott, 1990; Kilpatrick & Holland, 1990; Marty, 1980). Students need to understand their own spirituality in order to be able to effectively help clients grapple with these issues (Joseph, 1987; Kilpatrick & Holland). People often enter professional training programs and choose professions such as social work due to spiritual motivation (Gustafson, 1982; Prest & Russel, 1995). If social workers are going to help their clients to reach their fullest potential they need to use a spiritual perspective in practice (Cowley, 1993; Kilpatrick & Holland). In addition, a growing literature outside of the field of social work supports the efficacy of spiritually derived interventions such as prayer and meditation (e.g., Byrd, 1988; Dossey, 1993; Levey & Levey, 1991; Orme-Johnson, 1987). Social work educators are discussing the importance of training students in the use of these interventions (Canda, 1989; Sheridan et al., 1992).

The concepts of spirituality and religion have also been reintroduced into the Council on Social Work Education's curriculum guidelines. The Fourth Edition of the Council's Commission on Accreditation *Handbook of Accreditation Standards and Procedures* (1995) states that programs "must provide curriculum content about differences and similarities in the experiences, needs, and beliefs of people" (p. 140). Religion is mentioned as an element of client diversity that should be included in the curriculum. The Standards further provide that practice "content also includes approaches and skills for practice with clients from differing social, cultural, racial, religious, spiritual, and class backgrounds, and with systems of all sizes" (p. 141).

A number of recent studies have examined the attitudes of social work practitioners, educators and students toward spirituality and religion. Sheridan et al. (1992) surveyed a random sample of Virginia licensed clinical social workers, psychologists, and professional counselors on their attitudes and behaviors toward religion and spirituality. While the majority of subjects reported addressing religious and spiritual issues in their clinical practice, 79% indicated that these issues were rarely or never addressed in the course of their graduate education and training. Derezotes (1995) surveyed N.A.S.W. members in Utah and Idaho. The vast majority of respondents (94%) reported that they consider spiritual issues in practice and 76% indicated that they integrated spirituality into their practice. Only 27% of these subjects, however, said that they learned about how to integrate religious issues into their practice in their graduate education.

Two studies have examined the attitudes of social work educators toward the inclusion of religious and spiritual content in M.S.W. programs. Dudley and Helfgott (1990) surveyed the faculty of four schools of social work in two Eastern states. Seventy-five percent of the faculty agreed that spirituality is a fundamental aspect of being human. When asked if they would support the development of a course on spirituality and social work, 60% favored such a course as an elective and an additional 8% as a requirement. Yet, less than half of the respondents (47%) indicated that they thought that social workers should become more sophisticated in spiritual matters.

Sheridan, Wilmer, and Atcheson (1994) surveyed the population of full-time faculty at 25 accredited graduate social work programs in the southeastern United States about inclusion of religious and spiritual content in the M.S.W. curriculum. Generally, the respondents evidenced a "relatively positive or accepting attitude towards the role of religion and spirituality in practice" (p. 367). Interestingly, almost 89% of these faculty reported that content related to religious or spiritual issues was never or rarely presented in their graduate social work studies. As a group, they supported adding material on the spiritual dimension to the social work curriculum, with 82.5% of the respondents favoring the development of a specialized elective.

No national research exists on whether or how spiritual and religious issues are included in the M.S.W. curriculum. The literature does provide numerous recommendations of topics that should be included as part of graduate social work education. Commentators have advocated for inclusion of material on the stages of spiritual growth and development and how to assess functional and dysfunctional religious beliefs and experiences (Canda, 1989; Derezotes, 1995; Joseph, 1988; Sheridan et al., 1992). Students need to be exposed to diverse religious and spiritual beliefs and practices and taught the importance of respecting this diversity (Canda, 1989; Derezotes; Sheridan et al.). It has been suggested that students need the opportunity to explore their own spirituality in order to be able to effectively help clients with religious and spiritual issues (Canda,

1988b; Furman, 1994; Joseph, 1987; Sheridan et al.). It has also been argued that it is important to educate social work students about the role of sectarian agencies and religious congregations and about the interface with religious organizations in the policy arena (Netting et al., 1990; Sheridan et al.).

Spiritual and religious content can be introduced into the M.S.W. curriculum in two primary ways. The content can be integrated into existing M.S.W. courses, or courses can be developed that have a specific religious and/or spiritual focus. A number of authors have suggested methods for integrating spiritual and religious issues into existing courses (Canda, 1989; Cowley & Derezotes, 1994; Ortiz, 1991). And, there are published accounts of how two faculty have developed elective courses that highlight these issues (Furman, 1994; Krill, 1995).

DESCRIPTION OF THE RESEARCH PROJECT ON SPIRITUALITY COURSES AT M.S.W. PROGRAMS

An exploratory survey research project was conducted during 1995 for the purpose of describing the number and characteristics of courses on spirituality and/or religion being offered by M.S.W. programs in the United States. This research was conducted in two stages. Initially, a brief questionnaire was sent to all directors of the 118 M.S.W. programs accredited by the Council on Social Work Education. The instrument solicited demographic information about the program and about whether it offered a course on spirituality and/or religion as part of the graduate curriculum. If the school had such a course, directors were asked for the name, address and phone number of the faculty member teaching the course and for a copy of the course syllabus. If the school did not currently have such a course, directors were asked about whether such a course was being considered at their school.

Only 47 programs responded to the mailed survey. The remaining schools were contacted by telephone and the survey was administered to program directors or their designees. In this manner, completed surveys were obtained for 114 of the programs, a response rate of 96%.

Seventeen programs were identified as recently or currently offering graduate social work courses on spirituality and/or religion. A letter mailed to each faculty member identified as teaching these courses explained the purpose of the research and informed them that they would be contacted by telephone to be interviewed about their course. The brief questionnaire used for the telephone interviews of faculty included both closed-ended and open-ended questions about the history of the development of the course, student and peer reactions to the course, and their experiences teaching the course. Interviews were completed with 17 faculty members (one school had a course that was being team taught by two faculty members, and both were interviewed).

Course syllabi were obtained for 16 of the courses. A content analysis was performed on these syllabi, with particular attention to topics covered and texts utilized.

Responses to the initial survey revealed that 17 programs had separate courses on social work and spirituality and/or religion. Nine out of the 17 programs that have offered separate courses are located in the Midwest. Eight out of the 17 programs are at public schools, six are at private-sectarian institutions and three are at private-nonsectarian schools. Seven out of the 17 programs offering courses are located at Midwestern state universities.

The schools offering courses on social work and spirituality and/or religion are: Brigham Young University, Catholic University of America, College of St. Catherine/University of St. Thomas, Grand Valley State University, Our Lady of the Lake University of San Antonio, Smith College, St. Louis University, University of Cincinnati, University of Denver, University of Iowa, University of Kansas, University of Nebraska at Omaha, University of North Dakota, University of Utah, University of Wisconsin-Milwaukee, Walla Walla College, and Yeshiva University.

Separate courses on spirituality and/or religion are a relatively recent phenomenon. All but four of these courses were first developed within the last five years. Eight of the courses were first developed within the last two years. The oldest courses identified were developed 27 years ago at Yeshiva University, and 20 years ago at the Catholic University of America. Fourteen of the programs that do not currently offer courses on this topic, reported that there have been recent discussions at their schools about developing such a course.

The content analysis of the course syllabi revealed that a lot of variation existed in these courses in the areas of topics covered, texts or reading materials utilized, assignments and teaching modalities. Three of the courses focused almost exclusively on topics related to religion and social work. Two of the courses had a strong focus on transpersonal psychology. The remainder of the courses examined a combination of spiritual and religious issues.

The topics covered in the classes ranged from the historical religious/ spiritual roots of the social work profession to paranormal phenomena. There were, however, common topics that appeared on many of the syllabi. Table 1 reports the most commonly included topics and the number

TABLE 1. Common Topics Covered in Courses with Spiritual/Religious Foci

Topic (n = 16)	Number of Courses
Historical religious roots of the profession	10
Functional/dysfunctional aspects of religion and spirituality	10
Feminist perspectives/women's issues	10
Students' personal, spiritual and professional growth	9
Spiritually derived practice methods	8
Understanding and respecting spiritual diversity	8
Ethnic and other minority issues	8
Cooperation with religious and spiritual organizations	7
Developmental theories of spiritual and religious growth	7
Social action/social justice issues	7
Impact of belief systems on individuals and organizations	6
Religious perspectives on policy issues	5
Death and dying	4
Understanding the impact on practice of the social workers' belief system	4
Interface of religious and social work values	4
Working with spiritual issues in practice	4
Transpersonal theory and interventions	3
Working within religious organizations	3

of course syllabi that they appeared in. The topics most often found in the syllabi were: historical religious roots of the profession; the functional and dysfunctional aspects of clients' religious and spiritual beliefs and experiences; feminist spiritual perspectives and women's religious and spiritual issues; students' personal, spiritual and professional growth; spiritually derived practice methods; understanding and respecting spiritual diversity; ethnic and other minority issues; cooperation with religious and spiritual organizations; developmental theories of spiritual and religious growth; social action/social justice issues; and the impact of belief systems on individuals and organizations. Other infrequently reported topics included:

sociology of religion; experiences with U.F.O.s and aliens; use of tarot cards, rune stones and other methods of divination in social work practice; self-help recovery programs; gay and lesbian issues; responding to spiritual crises; past life regression therapy; and communicating with angels.

There was great variability in the 16 syllabi in reading assignments and texts listed. Six of the courses did not use a text book and relied instead on readings on reserve in the library or copied for students. These reading materials were primarily journal articles and chapters from books. In the other 10 courses there was little consistency in the selection of assigned texts. The most frequently assigned text was Loewenberg's *Religion and Social Work Practice in Contemporary American Society* (1988), and it was only used in three of the courses. There were only 2 texts that were assigned in two different courses: Lovinger's *Religion and Counseling: The Psychological Impact of Religious Belief* (1990) and Dass and Gorman's *How Can I Help?* (1985). Only 3 of the 25 different assigned texts were written by social workers.

Information received in telephone interviews with faculty revealed that in most instances the courses originated with the personal efforts of a faculty member who had a strong interest in the area. Some viewed developing the course as part of their own spiritual path. Most of the faculty had tenure at the time they developed the course. Their efforts in advocating for the course often followed a period of their own intensified spiritual growth. Usually the courses followed the route of first being offered on a one-time basis as a topical or experimental course. Repeat course offerings usually followed from very positive student evaluations and faculty and student advocacy on behalf of the course. At one school the course was initially developed due to student interest and advocacy.

The faculty reported that the biggest challenges they faced in developing the course were: overcoming their faculty colleagues' resistance and skepticism; narrowing the scope of material covered; and finding appropriate text books. Often colleague resistance stemmed from fear that a particular religious perspective would be presented in the class or that material presented would be considered to be "fuzzy," unprofessional, and inappropriate for graduate education. Interestingly, some of the faculty felt that they were able to overcome these objections because they taught research courses. This was perceived to give them some credibility as being "grounded." Some believed that their colleagues felt they "owed them" the opportunity to teach a course they found interesting since they taught the quantitative research courses that no one else in the department wanted to teach.

When faculty were asked about their personal goals for teaching these courses, the two most common responses were: to help students develop an awareness of the impact of spirituality on people's lives; and to help students in their own spiritual growth.

The respondents described a number of common challenges that they faced in the teaching of these courses. A basic challenge involved defining spirituality and religion so that students could distinguish between these two separate, but related, concepts. Another frequently described challenge involved maintaining a class-room environment that was respectful of spiritual and religious diversity. This involved keeping faculty persons' own personal beliefs and experiences from interfering with the maintenance of a neutral classroom environment, and dealing with students who were either prejudiced, closed minded or disrespectful of others' religious or spiritual beliefs and practices.

There also appeared to be great variability in the teaching methods utilized by the faculty. Faculty were asked about the percentages of class time devoted to lecture, class discussion and experiential learning. This information was obtained for 15 of the courses. The amount of class time spent in class discussion ranged from 25% to 75%, with a mean of 42%. The percentage of class time devoted to faculty or guest lectures ranged from 5% to 70%, with a mean of 33%. Class time spent in experiential learning ranged from none to 50%, with a mean of 25%.

Faculty described a rich variety of experiential learning experiences, including: visiting religious worship services; participating in a drumming circle; exploring spiritual beliefs through art work (e.g., students being given crayons and paper and told to draw pictures of their souls); developing class rituals; Sufi dancing; participating in a shamanic journey; learning to meditate; and exploring past life experiences through relaxation and visualization.

Faculty indicated that student evaluations of the courses were extremely positive. They were asked in the telephone interviews "on a scale of 1 to 10, with 1 being the least favorable and 10 the most favorable, how favorable were the evaluations?" Reported student evaluation scores, available for 14 of the courses, ranged from 8 to 10, with a mean evaluation score of 9.27. Faculty for 9 of the 14 courses reported evaluations of 9.5 or better. Often these high student evaluations and student support and advocacy were instrumental in school decisions to continue to offer these courses.

Most of the faculty reported that this was their favorite course to teach. The faculty were also asked to identify what they found to be most personally rewarding about teaching this course. The most common responses were: the high degree of student interest and their positive response to the course; observing students better integrate their personal and professional lives; experiencing student creativity; providing an environment in which students shared with each other their personal growth and learned from each others' experiences; the sense of community that often developed in these classes; and the personal learning of the professor.

It is difficult to describe adequately the passion and commitment evidenced by the faculty when they talked about these courses. It was evident in the interviews that the spirituality course was not just one more assignment on a faculty member's academic load. Many of the faculty had invested much energy in getting approval to develop the course in the first place. Numerous faculty described how developing and teaching these courses allowed them to better integrate their spiritual and work worlds. They also described their hopes that these courses would facilitate the same integration for students.

DISCUSSION

The results of this survey demonstrate a recent trend in the development of elective social work courses with a focus on spirituality and religion in M.S.W. programs. During the six months since the survey was completed the author has received requests from faculty at seven programs for assistance in developing syllabi for spirituality courses at their schools. Two of those courses were slated to be offered during the spring semester of 1996.

Clearly, the interface between spirituality, religion, and social work is beginning to be more widely viewed as a legitimate focus of study in M.S.W. programs. This is supported by the new accreditation standards of the Council on Social Work Education. This research strongly suggests that faculty and students are having very positive experiences in the elective courses being offered in this area.

There is much variation in the courses being offered with a religious or spiritual focus. While many courses are covering the areas of knowledge recommended by the literature, emphasis seems to vary with the interests and expertise of the faculty. One would hope that some of this variance is also reflective of differences in the client community and student body in the areas where the schools are located. Because this is a relatively new area of curriculum development, schools and faculty interested in developing new courses on spirituality and religion may need assistance in developing course syllabi. In the past few years, the Council on Social Work Education has sponsored a Faculty Development Institute on this topic at their Annual Program Meetings. And, the Society for Spirituality and

Social Work developed a syllabus resource packet for interested faculty (Herzog & Russel, 1995). These are steps in the right direction.

The faculty who were interviewed expressed difficulty with finding texts to use in these courses. This was also reflected in the wide range of primarily non-social work books being assigned and in the substantial number of faculty who did not assign texts at all. It is time for some of our social work scholars and practitioners with an interest in this area to develop texts that can be used in social work courses. The growing number of courses being developed with spiritual and religious focus would certainly substantiate the potential market for such a text. A well conceived and written text that responds to the educational needs highlighted in the literature would also assist faculty developing such a course for the first time.

Instructors who teach electives in spirituality need to pay special attention to a few key issues. It is imperative that the instructor model tolerance and appreciation for spiritual diversity and dialogue (Canda, 1989). The classroom must be a safe place where students can freely explore and express their beliefs, experiences, and feelings about spirituality and religion. Dialogue involves the affirmation of differences and commonalities between people. As the interviews of faculty teaching these courses revealed, often, the most difficult students for the instructor to accept are those who themselves are not tolerant of spiritual diversity.

This study found that the majority of the faculty interviewed used some experiential teaching methods in these courses. A substantial number of the exercises described by the faculty involved various means of entering altered or focused states of consciousness through meditation or visualization techniques. Not all students may be open to or ready for these experiences. Voluntary participation and a nonjudgmental faculty attitude about nonparticipation are essential. Faculty also need to be alert to the risks inherent in leading students into these experiences.

Social work students are often survivors of childhood trauma and are in various stages of healing when they enter M.S.W. programs (Black, Jeffreys & Hartley, 1993; Russel, Gill, Coyne & Woody, 1993). Spirituality has been found to be a powerful tool in helping survivors make sense of painful early life experiences and may also play a role in propelling them into the helping professions (Sanford, 1990). It is not unreasonable to expect that a student who is a survivor of early trauma would feel an attraction to a class on spirituality. Faculty teaching these courses need to be particularly sensitive to these issues, especially when using experiential exercises in class that may bring about recall of traumatic events or cathartic expressions of feelings.

Research on spirituality and social work is in its infancy and has primarily focused on the attitudes and practices of social work practitioners and educators. Research is needed on the impact of including the spiritual dimension in practice as well as on the efficacy of spiritually derived interventions. We need to learn which interventions work best with particular presenting problems and types of clients. Social workers also have an ethical obligation to make sure that their interventions do not harm clients. But as Canda (1988a) suggested, strategies for research and evaluation of practice "need to be developed that are sensitive to the spiritual aspects of clients' experiences without reducing spirituality to superficial measurable expressions" (p. 44).

Courses on spirituality, religion and social work may be among the most popular for students and the faculty teaching them. Perhaps this new area of curriculum development also reflects society's growing hunger for spirituality. The problems facing clients, practitioners, local and global communities are becoming increasingly complex. Courses with spiritual and religious focus may seem, to some, to be offering new solutions. In rediscovering professional roots, however, students and educators are reclaiming the heart and soul of social work and being given the opportunity to resacralize their work.

REFERENCES

Black, P.N., Jeffreys, D. & Hartley, E.K. (1993). Personal history of psychosocial trauma in the early life of social work and business students. *Journal of Social Work Education, 29*(2), 171-180.

Byrd, R.C. (1988). Positive therapeutic effects of intercessory prayer in a coronary care unit population. *Southern Medical Journal, 81*(7), 826-829.

Canda, E.R. (1988a). Conceptualizing spirituality for social work: Insights from diverse perspectives. *Social Thought, 14*(1), 30-46.

Canda, E.R. (1988b). Spirituality, religious diversity, and social work practice. *Social Casework, 69,* 238-247.

Canda, E.R. (1989). Religious content in social work education: A comparative approach. *Journal of Social Work Education, 25*(1), 36-45.

Canda, E.R. (1995, Fall). Retrieving the soul of social work. *Society for Spirituality and Social Work Newsletter, 2,* 5-8.

Council on Social Work Education. (1953). Curriculum policy statement. *Manual of Accrediting Standards.* New York: Council on Social Work Education.

Council on Social Work Education Commission on Accreditation. (1995). *Handbook of accreditation standards and procedures.* Alexandria, VA: Council on Social Work Education.

Cowley, A.S. (1993). Transpersonal social work: A theory for the 1990s, *Social Work, 38*(5), 527-534.

Cowley, A.S. & Derezotes, D. (1994). Transpersonal psychology and social work education. *Journal of Social Work Education, 30*(1), 32-41.

Dass, R. & Gorman, P. (1985). *How can I help?* New York: Alfred A. Knopf.

Denton, R.T. (1990). The religiously fundamentalist family: Training for assessment and treatment. *Journal of Social Work Education, 26*(1), 6-14.

Derezotes, D.S. (1995). Spirituality and religiosity: Neglected factors in social work practice. *Arete, 20*(1), 1-15.

Dossey, L. (1993). *Healing words: The power of prayer and the practice of medicine.* New York: Harper Collins Publishers.

Dudley, J.R. & Helfgott, C. (1990). Exploring a place for spirituality in the social work curriculum. *Journal of Social Work Education, 26*(3), 287-294.

Furman, L.E. (1994). Religion and spirituality in social work education: Preparing the culturally-sensitive practitioner for the future. *Social Work & Christianity: An International Journal, 21*(2), 103-117.

Gustafson, J.M. (1982). Professions as "callings." *Social Service Review, 56*(4), 501-515.

Herzog, S. & Russel, R. (1995, Fall). Spirituality courses in M.S.W. programs. *Society for Spirituality and Social Work Newsletter, 2,* 1-2.

Holland, T.P. (1989). Values, faith and professional practice. *Social Thought, 15*(1), 28-40.

Imre, R.W. (1984). The nature of knowledge in social work. *Social Work, 29*(1), 41-45.

Joseph, M.V. (1987). The religious and spiritual aspects of clinical practice: A neglected dimension of social work. *Social Thought, 13*(1), 12-23.

Joseph, M.V. (1988). Religion and social work practice. *Social Casework, 60*(7), 443-452.

Kilpatrick, A.C. & Holland, T.P. (1990). Spiritual dimensions of practice. *The Clinical Supervisor, 8*(2), 125-140.

Krill, D.F. (1995). My spiritual sojourn into existential social work. *Reflections, 1*(4), 57-64.

Leiby, J. (1985). Moral foundations of social welfare and social work: A historical view. *Social Work, 30*(4), 323-330.

Levey, J. & Levey, M. (1991). *Quality of mind.* Boston, MA: Wisdom Publications.

Loewenberg, F.M. (1988). *Religion and social work practice in contemporary American society.* New York: Columbia University Press.

Lovinger, R.J. (1990). *Religion and counseling: The psychological impact of religious belief.* New York: Continuum.

Marshall, J. (1991). The spiritual dimension in social work education. *Spirituality and Social Work Communicator, 2*(1), 12-15.

Marty, M.E. (1980). Social service: Godly or Godless. *Social Service Review, 54*(4), 463-481.

Netting, F.E., Thibault, J.M., & Ellor, J.W. (1990). Integrating content on organized religion into macropractice courses. *Journal of Social Work Education, 26*(1), 15-24.

Orme-Johnson, D. (1987). Medical care utilization rates in the transcendental meditation program. *Journal of Psychosomatic Medicine, 49*, 493-507.

Prest, L.A. & Russel, R. (1995, November). *Spirituality in training, practice, & personal development.* Poster session presented at the annual meeting of the American Association for Marriage and Family Therapy, Baltimore, MD.

Roof, W.C. (1993). *A generation of seekers: The spiritual journeys of the baby boom generation.* New York: Harper Collins Publishers.

Russel, R., Gill, P., Coyne, A. & Woody, J. (1993). Dysfunction in the family of origin of MSW and other graduate students. *Journal of Social Work Education, 29*(1), 121-129.

Sanford, L.T. (1990). *Strong at the broken places.* New York: Random House.

Sermabeikian, P. (1994). Our clients, ourselves: The spiritual perspective and social work practice. *Social Work, 39*(2), 178-183.

Sheridan, M.J., Bullis, R.K., Adcock, C.R., Berlin, S.D., & Miller, P.C. (1992). Practitioners' personal and professional attitudes and behaviors toward religion and spirituality: Issues for education and practice. *Journal of Social Work Education, 28*(2), 190-203.

Sheridan, M.J., Wilmer, C.M., & Atcheson, L. (1994). Inclusion of content on religion and spirituality in the social work curriculum: A study of faculty views. *Journal of Social Work Education, 30*(3), 363-376.

Siporin, M. (1982). Moral philosophy in social work today. *Social Service Review, 56*(4), 516-538.

Siporin, M. (1985). Current social work perspectives on clinical practice. *Clinical Social Work Journal, 13*, 198-217.

Siporin, M. (1986). Contribution of religious values to social work and the law. *Social Thought, 12*(4), 35-50.

Spencer, S.W. (1956). Religion and social work. *Social Work, 1*, 19-26.

Spencer, S.W. (1961). What place has religion in social work education? *Social Service Review, 35*, 161-170.

An Exploration of Intuition
for Social Work Practice and Education

Barbara B. Luoma

SUMMARY. Intuition, the "first awareness," is present before thought engages and is always at our service. Although intuition is rarely a specific focus in the social work literature, it is receiving increasing attention in many fields. It is time for intuition to be investigated for its possible contribution to the field of social work. This article discusses an evolving context for intuition found in the literature on the spiritual dimension in social work practice, transpersonal theory, and practice wisdom. It also reports the results of an exploratory investigation of social work students' attitude toward intuition. They were highly positive about the existence of intuition and the importance of studying the intuitive capacity of the human being in order to enhance social work practice. *[Article copies available for a fee from The Haworth Document Delivery Service: 1-800-342-9678. E-mail address: getinfo@haworthpressinc.com]*

INTRODUCTION

My experience using intuition as a deliberate and integral element in social work practice and education has encouraged me to investigate the

Barbara B. Luoma, ACSW, CMSW, is Consultant on Organizational Change, 319 Bee Knob Road, Whittier, NC 28789. She gratefully acknowledges the assistance of Patrick A. Hays, Associate Professor of Finance, Department of Economics, Finance, and International Business, Western Carolina University, who performed the statistical analysis and interpreted the results.

[Haworth co-indexing entry note]: "An Exploration of Intuition for Social Work Practice and Education." Luoma, Barbara B. Co-published simultaneously in *Social Thought* (The Haworth Pastoral Press, an imprint of The Haworth Press, Inc.) Vol. 18, No. 2, 1998, pp. 31-45; and: *Spirituality in Social Work: New Directions* (ed: Edward R. Canda) The Haworth Pastoral Press, an imprint of The Haworth Press, Inc., 1998, pp. 31-45. Single or multiple copies of this article are available for a fee from The Haworth Document Delivery Service [1-800-342-9678, 9:00 a.m. - 5:00 p.m. (EST). E-mail address: getinfo@haworthpressinc.com].

literature on this subject as well as explore the practical implications. Fields such as education, medicine, law, and business, to name just a few, have increasingly examined and acknowledged the value of intuition. However, only recently have professionals been willing to acknowledge its importance as a tool in their specific fields. One might expect that social work would have a particular interest in this topic, yet rarely is intuition a direct focus in the social work literature (Eichler & Halseth, 1992).

This paper is divided into three parts. It first examines briefly the historical background of the concept of intuition, along with some of the current relevant literature in the fields of psychology, education, business, and medicine. Next a professional context for intuition is established by a review of recent social work literature that bears on the subject. Finally, the results of an exploratory study of students' perception of intuition are presented and analyzed. The aim of this paper is to invite social work to increase its attention in this arena so that the relevance of intuition may be identified, supported, and enhanced.

REVIEW OF THE LITERATURE

Intuition is defined as "the act or process of coming to direct knowledge or certainty without reasoning or inferring" (*Webster's New International Dictionary*, 1993 ed., p. 1887). According to Imbrogno and Canda (1988) ". . . it is a non-rational grasping of the whole . . . and goes beyond the rational analytic decomposition of systems" (p. 23).

Intuition is certainly not a new concept. It has engaged the attention of such minds as Aristotle (384-322 BC), Descartes (1596-1650), Spinoza (1632-1677), Kant (1724-1804), and Bergson (1859-1941), to name a few, who have grappled with describing, defining and comprehending intuition (Summers, 1976). It has been acknowledged for its role in human evolution (Salk, 1993; Cappon 1993) and has certainly been honored the world over for its contribution to scientific discovery (Sorokin, 1957; Sullivan, 1992). Daniel Cappon calls it the "archetypical jewel in the crown of human intelligence." A great believer in rational thought, he is convinced that "intuition is the older, wiser and perhaps greater part of human intelligence" (Cappon, 1993, pp. 40-41).

Pitirim Sorokin, author of *The Crisis of Our Age*, emphasizes its importance in the following statement:

> [T]here is hardly any doubt that intuition is the real source of knowledge different from the role of the senses and reason. It is

especially indispensable in the apprehension of those aspects of reality which are inaccessible to the senses and to reason. (Mishlove, 1994, p. 32)

Sorokin (1941), in discussing the impact on our society of the emphasis on reason and sensing as our source of knowledge, feels we need a different approach to accessing knowledge in order to respond to the crisis we face in our society.

The transpersonal theorist, Ken Wilber (1993), makes a strong case for intuition, calling it the non-dual mode of knowing. He describes the two ways of knowing as symbolic or representational thought and knowing immediately or intuitively. "To know intuitively or immediately is for mental content and object to be identical" (Wilber, 1993, p. 33). This way of knowing is aimed at the understanding of life directly instead of in the abstract. Intuition is an important key in our efforts to perceive reality and to add to our comprehension of human existence (Wilber, 1993).

Intuition in Related Fields

Intuition is currently receiving increased attention in many fields. Psychology has chosen to examine the psychological aspects and the type of person considered to be intuitive. Malcom Wescott (1968) described a portrait of an intuitive personality. This corresponded with Jungian data on the intuitive type "and both fit well with data on problem-solving styles and with measures of qualities associated with intuitive people–creativity, originality, and independence of judgement" (Goldberg, 1983, p. 109).

> Jung's conceptual framework of thinking, feeling, sensing, and intuiting guided the work of Myers & Briggs, who developed the Myers-Briggs Type Indicator (1962, 1980) as a means of determining a person's Jungian type. Current interest by individuals and organizations on learning more about temperament types or psychological styles can be traced back to Jung. (Halseth, 1988, pp. 29-30)

In education, the importance of intuition has been explored as a significant factor by Noddings and Sore (1984). Their research found that intuition is driven by the will's quest for meaning. For the purpose of education it is best to describe intuitive activity in the form of intuitive modes ". . . characterized by the commitment of the will, receptivity, involvement of the senses, the quest for understanding, and a tension between subjective certainty and objective uncertainty" (Noddings & Sore, 1984, p. 202). Although Noddings and Sore focused their investigation on the role of intuition in intellectual activity from the perspective of education, they add that it may be worthwhile to carry out a close examination of intuitive activity in other domains, especially the moral domain.

> When moral situations are approached intuitively, we refuse to 'think' the persons we engage; instead, we encounter them directly— we receive them, feel what they feel, and put our motivational energies into their service. The field of moral education is virtually sterile today, completely dominated by approaches that rely almost entirely on reason and logic. (p. 203)

Intuition has perhaps received the most attention in business where its applications in management and decision making are being recognized. Inspired by the work of Weston Agor (1986) who, in a study of 3,000 executives, identified a connection between financial success of a corporation and the intuitive management style of its chief executive officer, intuition became an acknowledged part of corporate decision making. Agor found that in 1974 an executive would not admit to the use of intuition. By 1980, supported by advances in quantum physics and the understanding of the interconnectedness between all things, this cautious attitude began to change. Roy Rowan (1986) talks about avoiding "analysis paralysis" by using intuition to dip into "some kind of shared cosmic pool [since] there is an energy link between everything in the universe" (p. 99).

In decision making and in management, intuition has become an area of specialized training (Agor, 1986; Sullivan; 1992, Schultz, 1994).

> As consultants, employees, and executives invite intuition and inner wisdom into factories, laboratories, and corporate offices, they are reaping the rewards of enhanced creativity, accelerated decision making, increased productivity, and more authentic communication. (Schultz, 1994, p. 15)

The Intuition Network, housed with the Institute of Noetic Sciences (a research, education, and membership organization), is playing a vital role in supporting research and the networking of those focused on bringing intuition into the workplace as well as into the personal arena. Included in the Network statement of purpose is the emphasis on "creating a world in which people feel encouraged to rely on their inner resources" (Noetic Science Bulletin, 1994/1995). Publications, conferences, and organizations supporting the utilization of intuition are multiplying rapidly.

Medicine is utilizing an understanding of intuition in various approaches, especially in the non-traditional methods of healing (Borysenko, 1984; Chopra, 1987a, 1990b; Ingerman, 1991; Northrup, 1994; Rew, 1986; Winter, 1988). For instance, research about cancer treatments has taken advantage of the applications of intuition to assist in the individual's healing process (Simonton, Simonton & Creighton, 1981).

Advances in quantum physics continue to open new doors. "Physicists, psychologists, and molecular biologists are intrigued with the possibility that everything that happens is simultaneously encoded everywhere" (Rowan, 1986, p. 99). This concept has powerful implications. Rupert Sheldrake, a British biologist, says "whenever a member of a species learns something new, the 'causative field' or behavioral blueprint is altered. Then, if the new behavior is repeated enough, a 'morphic resonance' is established that will affect every member of the species" (Rowan, 1986, p. 102). These concepts certainly invite a reconsideration of current conventional beliefs. Willis Harmon (1995) calls intuition the "code word for global transformation."

Intuition in Social Work

"It is important to accept the fact that social workers engage in intuition consciously or unconsciously, and it has become a vital part of social work practice" (Imbrogno & Canda, 1988, p. 24). It is time to acknowledge this potential asset that in the past may have been underestimated, underutilized, and discussed only indirectly in the social work literature. In addition, it is important to point out that the intuitive mode or way of knowing needs to complement and be integrated with rational analysis.

In the recent literature, there appears to be an evolving context for intuition in discussions on the following topics: (1) the importance of the spiritual dimension in social work practice (Canda, 1988a, 1988b; Dudley & Helfgott, 1990; Cornett, 1992); (2) the role of transpersonal approaches to social work (Wilber, 1993; Cowley, 1993; Cowley & Derezotes, 1994); (3) practice wisdom as it bridges the gap between empirical and theoretical knowledge (Krill, 1990; Klein & Bloom, 1995), (4) creativity (Harmon & Rheingold, 1984), and (5) empathy (Raines, 1990).

Intuition may be considered the first awareness which is nonrational in nature and present before thought engages. Therefore it can always be at our service. Intuition may be the brain/mind capacity possessed by all people which makes possible direct knowing. It may be the capability by which the social worker accesses information not tapped by conventional analytic means. It is this capability that may facilitate the transition into the future of social work practice in which an expanded level of consciousness will include the spiritual dimension and allow space for growth in yet unidentified ways.

> Whether the evolution of consciousness within the individual or society takes place in the years ahead will depend to a large degree on the belief systems that shape and guide us. Premises held by our society and those in the helping professions about human possibilities and the upper limits of psychological well-being will help determine our future as a species. (Cowley, 1993, p. 533)

In the search for ways to become more conscious, to become more fully human, Wilber's Full Spectrum Model (adapted by Cowley and Derezotes, 1994) adds a transpersonal, transrational level of development, to the understanding of the human being. "The transpersonal perspective offers an expanded notion of human possibilities that goes beyond self-actualization and, beyond ego" (Cowley and Derezotes, 1994, p. 34). A larger transpersonal understanding of human nature needs to be incorporated into the practice of social work as well as into the educational process to be passed on to the next wave of future social workers. For this task, intuition may be the most appropriate tool.

In the implementation of Wilber's Full Spectrum Model which considers various levels of consciousness, associated forms of mental health and pathology, and therapeutic interventions (Cowley, 1993), intuition seems to be the tool of choice. Cowley suggests that by including the transpersonal dimension ". . . Wilber opened up a source of wisdom that has been belittled by science because of its transrational nature. Wilber contends that the focus in Western traditions on linear, left hemisphere, empirical evidence has tended to deny the validity of intuitive and mystical experience" (Cowley, 1993, p. 532).

As already suggested, practice wisdom may offer another arena which provides a potential language for the exploration of the role of intuition. Klein and Bloom (1995) define it as "a personal and value driven system of knowledge that emerges out of the transaction between the phenomenological experience of the client situation and the use of scientific information" (p. 799). Practice wisdom allows the development of professionally guided interventions that include feelings, insights, values and supports the translations between two systems of knowing. "Practice wisdom is a significant component of both quantitative and qualitative knowledge and thus links empirical knowledge and practice" (Klein & Bloom, 1995, p. 803).

The importance of an expanded view of human nature cannot be underestimated. "For social work practice and social work education to remain relevant to the social problems of our day, the spiritual dimension can no longer be ignored or left as a missing or neglected dimension" (Cowley, 1993, p. 533). For both the social work professional and the recipient of professional assistance, intuition can become a critical tool in the process of accessing more of the self to provide a more comprehensive approach to the issues being presented.

It is important to note that just as the professional adapts therapeutic interventions to the level of functioning of the client, Wilber's Full Spectrum Model suggests adapting interventions to the level of consciousness of the client (Cowley & Derezotes, 1994). This may simply be another way of saying that the professional "goes to where the client is." In this case it adds the awareness of the spiritual dimension. Clearly, the ability to include the spiritual domain of the client is essential in making effective assessments and proceeding with appropriate interventions where once again intuition can be invaluable.

SOCIAL WORK STUDENTS' PERCEPTIONS OF INTUITION

Given the promise of intuition for enhancing social work practice, an approach for educating students about intuition was developed at the Department of Social Work and Sociology of Western Carolina University, and students' perceptions of intuition were evaluated by the author. Initially, intuition was discussed in the first practice course in an undergraduate social work program. Students were extremely fascinated by this initial exposure and requested additional training. This led to a weekend intensive course (15 hours–1 credit hour) during the spring of 1994 on the applications of intuition and has continued as an annual course offering.

These teaching experiences prompted a more formal investigation of students' perceptions of intuition. Answers were sought to such questions as: Were students aware of intuition and its role? And, if so, what were their perceptions about it?

Methodology

A questionnaire was designed based on the research carried out by B. Truax (1985). Students were asked to respond to a selected number of items about their perceptions of intuition according to a scale from 1 (no/least/never/disagree strongly) to 10 (yes/most/always/agree strongly). The statements focused on some basic aspects of intuition as follows:

1. I believe intuition exists.
2. I would describe myself as an intuitive person.

3. I utilize intuition in my daily life.
4. I use intuition in decision making.
5. I believe intuition is trustworthy.
6. I believe that we should study the intuitive capacity of the brain.
7. I have been able to validate my intuitions.
8. I am interested in discovering more ways to improve my intuition.

Students were asked to provide their personal definition or list words and phrases they associate with intuition. Although they differed in their specific descriptors, it was clear that they recognized the non-rational nature of intuition. Such words as gut feeling, hunch, insight, knowing-ness, inner voice, knowing without logical information, an understanding of the intangible, to know without knowing how you know, were the most common definitions provided. Clearly additional work in defining intuition for the social work student and the social work practitioner needs to occur.

This questionnaire was administered to five social work classes and one sociology class in the fall of 1994 and the spring of 1995. The sample was divided into 3 groups. Group 1 consisted of the intensive workshop class on intuition and was labeled the 'intensive' exposure sample. Group 2 was labeled as the 'some exposure' sample and consisted of three social work classes that were exposed to intuition as part of the content of the course. Group 3 was a 'control' group comprised of one sociology and one social work class where there was no formal mention of, or exposure to, intuition.

The total sample consisted of 99 respondents who were present for both the beginning and end of semester questionnaires broken down as follows: 10 in group 1, 51 in group 2, and 38 in group 3. The results for another intensive workshop class, held in the spring of 1994, will be reported separately because a slightly different questionnaire was utilized.

The statistic that was chosen to measure the consistency of the relative agreement between the respondents' perceptions about intuition was Kendall's tau, or tau-b. This measure is appropriate for the ranked, or scaled, data in this questionnaire (Liebetrau, 1983; Daniel, 1990). The tau-b compares the responses to two statements by a given student to the corresponding responses from all other students in a sample. All possible combinations of pairs of rankings are compared to find the number of concordant and discordant pairs. Since the tau-b value would equal 1 if all paired comparisons were concordant and equal -1 if all paired comparisons were discordant, this measure has the attributes of the other standard correlation, or association, measures.

Analysis of the Questionnaire

As a first step, it seems appropriate to establish whether the respondents believe in the concept of intuition. Figure 1 shows the frequency of responses, on a scale of 1 to 10, for the statement "I believe that intuition exists." The number of responses above a level of 6 (indicating agreement) to the statement that intuition exists was 92 out of the 99 total participants. This 93% positive response rate strongly suggests that students in all three groups believed that intuition exists. The responses were extremely positive, or higher on the rating scale, for groups 1 and 2 that were exposed to intuition in the class. However, the responses from control group 3 were also very positive. For groups 1 and 2, the number of responses in the very positive range (8-10 on the rating scale) was 55 of 64 or 86%. For group 3, the number in the very positive range was 24 of 35 or about 69%. Certainly these percentages of very positive responses were remarkably high for all groups. This strong belief in the existence of intuition was utilized as a base for studying students' perceptions about

FIGURE 1

BAR CHART FOR ALL 3 GROUPS
Q1: I Believe That Intuition Exists

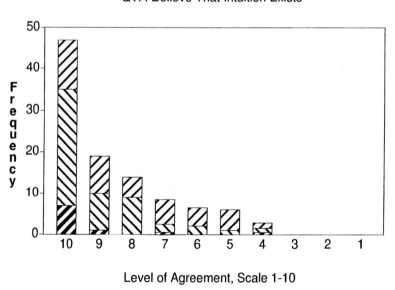

Level of Agreement, Scale 1-10

G1   G2   G3

intuition. From the figures in Panel A of Table 1, several common patterns emerged with respect to the degree of concordance between the questionnaire statements and the exposure to intuition in class. In every case, the concordance between the belief that intuition exists and the statements about intuition were, as expected, a direct function of the level of the exposure to intuition in class; that is, it was highest for group 1, lower for group 2, and lowest for group 3.

There was a highly significant concordance between the belief in the existence of intuition and whether the respondents perceived themselves to be intuitive. In fact, the proportion of consistent responses had less variance between groups for these statements than for any of the other statements. The groups exposed to intuition in class responded they had been able to validate intuition and believed it was trustworthy in a manner consistent with their level of belief that intuition exists. For the control group, the concordances between these statements were not significant.

The stronger the belief that intuition exists, the higher the level of interest in discovering more ways to improve intuition. This relationship was noticeably higher for the groups exposed to intuition in class. The correlation between these statements was low for the control group, although it was significant. All three groups indicated that the intuitive capacity of the brain should be studied and their responses were consistent with the intensity of their belief in intuition.

A belief that intuition exists did not necessarily mean that students thought they used intuition in their daily lives. Only group 1 had a significant concordance between the belief that intuition exists and the perception that it was used in daily life. Thus, the statements about the use of intuition in daily life and in decision making seemed to be specifically related to whether the respondents perceived themselves to be "an intuitive person." The correspondence between these statements and the degree of intuition that a person is perceived to have is shown in Panel B of Table 1.

For groups 1 and 2, the stronger the students' perception that they were intuitive, the more they thought they utilized intuition in their daily lives. For the control group, the responses were actually discordant at a reasonably significant level. The stronger the students' belief that they were intuitive, the more likely they were to use intuition to make decisions. The correlation between these perceptions about intuition was highly dependent on the exposure to intuition in class.

TABLE 1

Panel A

Kendall's Measure of Concordance Between the belief that intuition exists and the belief that:					
I'm an intuitive person			intuition is trustworthy		
Group	Tau value	Probability	Group	Tau value	Probability
1	0.536	.016	1	0.759	.001
2	0.523	.000	2	.0557	.000
3	0.416	.000	3	0.177	.067
study our intuitive capacity			been able to validate intuition		
Group	Tau value	Probability	Group	Tau value	Probability
1	0.667	.004	1	0.510	.020
2	0.472	.000	2	0.468	.000
3	0.409	.000	3	0.143	.144
discover ways to improve intuition					
Group		Tau value		Probability	
1		0.842		.001	
2		0.527		.000	
3		0.249		.018	

Panel B

Kendall's Measure of Concordance Between the statement "I would describe myself as an intuitive person" and the belief that:					
intuition used in my daily life			intuition used in decision making		
Group	Tau value	Probability	Group	Tau value	Probability
1	0.795	.001	1	0.781	.001
2	0.338	.000	2	0.473	.000
3	−0.184	.060	3	0.285	.008

Prior Intensive Workshop Results

The results from an intensive class on intuition held in February 1994 are now reported separately. Although the statements about intuition were essentially the same as those in Table 1, the format of the questionnaire given to this class was different. All 20 of the valid responses from this class selected the highest level of agreement (a value of 10) to the statement "I believe that intuition exists." The fact that these students chose this class after an initial exposure to intuition as part of course content might explain why all 20 students in this class responded with the highest value. These extremely positive responses to the existence of intuition are consistent with, and slightly higher than, the rankings from group 1.

Table 2 shows the concordances between the belief that intuition exists and the perceptions about intuition. All of them are significant and tend to confirm the results for group 1 in Table 1. Also, like group 1, the use of intuition in their daily lives and in decision making was a direct function of how strongly respondents perceived themselves to be intuitive. The similarity of responses from this intuition workshop class to the responses

TABLE 2

Panel A

Kendall's Measure of Concordance Between the "belief that intuition exists" and the belief that:		
Statement	Tau value	Probability
I'm an intuitive person	0.308	.025
intuition is trustworthy	0.415	.004
study our intuitive capacity	0.592	.000
discover ways to improve intuition	0.716	.000

Panel B:

Kendall's Measure of Concordance Between the statement "I would describe myself as an intuitive person" and the belief that:		
Statement	Tau value	Probability
intuition used in daily life	0.692	.000
intuition used in decision making	0.814	.000

from group 1 strongly supports the findings related to an "intensive" exposure to intuition in class.

Summary of the Analysis

The analysis of a questionnaire given to students in several classes in the department of social work and sociology produced some interesting results regarding their perceptions about intuition. By their extremely positive responses, participants strongly indicated that they believed intuition exists. The perceptions about intuition for the groups exposed to intuition in class were generally consistent with their belief in intuition. The perceptions about intuition for the control group not exposed to intuition in class were, as expected, not as concordant with their belief in intuition.

Also, groups 1 and 2 believed more strongly that they were intuitive and, therefore, used intuition in their daily lives as well to make decisions. The responses from group 3 about the use of intuition were relatively inconsistent with their perceptions of being an intuitive person.

More importantly, all groups were interested in improving their intuition and believed that the intuitive capacity of the brain/mind should be studied. This is a significant finding since exposure to intuition in class increased the concordance between respondents' belief in intuition and their perceptions about intuition.

CONCLUSION

This article proposes that intuition, long present implicitly in social work practice, needs to be investigated for its potential contribution to the social work field. Although intuition as a subject is rarely addressed explicitly in the social work literature, it is currently receiving extensive attention in many fields. Within social work, increasing discussion on spirituality, transpersonal social work, and practice wisdom provides a context heretofore lacking for the exploration of intuition in this profession.

The analysis of students' responses to questionnaire statements about intuition produced several important findings. There was a remarkably high proportion of extremely positive responses, directly related to the degree of exposure to intuition in class, which indicated a strong belief in the existence of intuition. The participants were interested in discovering more ways to improve their intuition and wanted to study the intuitive capacity of the human being.

It is hoped that this article has made a case for intuition and will encourage further investigation. Not only is it time for intuition to be an equal partner with logic and reason, it is essential to combine both for an integrated approach to understanding ourselves and the world in which we live.

REFERENCES

Agor, W. (1986). *The logic of intuitive decision making.* Westport, CT: Greenwood Press, Inc.

Appleton, E. (1994). Woman to woman (Christine Northrup, MD). *New Age Journal.* Nov/Dec, 60-65, 140, 142-144.

Borysenko, J. (1984). *Minding the body, mending the mind.* Reading: Addison-Wesley Publishing Co., Inc.

Canda, E. R. (1988a). Spirituality, religious diversity and social work practice. *Social Casework: The Journal of Contemporary Social Work, 69* (4), 238-247.

Canda, E. R. (1988b). Conceptualizing spirituality for social work: Insights from diverse perspectives. *Social Thought, 14* (1), 30-46.

Cappon, D. (1993). The anatomy of intuition. *Psychology Today, 26* (3), 40-45.

Chopra, D. (1990). *Quantum healing: Exploring the frontiers of mind/body healing.* New York: Bantam Books.

Chopra, D. (1987). *Creating health: Beyond prevention toward perfection.* Boston: Houghton Mifflin Company.

Cornett, C. (1992). Toward a more comprehensive personology: Integrating a spiritual perspective into social work practice. *Social Work, 37* (2), 101-102.

Cowley, A. S. (1993). Transpersonal social work: A theory for the 1990s. *Social Work, 38* (5), 527-534.

Cowley, A. S. & Derezotes, D. (1994). Transpersonal psychology and social work education. *Journal of Social Work Education, 26* (1), 32-41.

Daniel, Wayne W. (1990). *Applied nonparametric statistics.* Boston, MA: PWS-Kent Publishers.

Dudley, J. R. & Helfgott, G. (1990). Exploring a place for spirituality in the social work curriculum. *Journal of Social Work Education, 26* (3), 287-294.

Eichler, R. L. & Halseth, J. H. (1992). Intuition: Enhancing group work. *Social Work with Groups, 15* (1), 81-93.

Goldberg, P. (1983). *The intuitive edge.* Los Angeles: Jeremy P. Tarcher, Inc.

Halseth, G. H. (1988). Intuition in decision making by human service administrators. (Doctoral dissertation, Western Michigan University, Kalamazoo, 1988/1989.) *Dissertation Abstract International, 50,* (2), 483-A.

Harmon, W. W. (1988). Intuition as the code word for global transformation. IMI Conference on Intuition in Business, Geneva, February 19, 1988.

Harmon, W. & Rheingold, H. (1984). *Higher creativity: Liberating the unconscious for breakthrough insights.* Los Angeles: Jeremy P. Tarcher, Inc.

Imbrogno, S. & Canda, E. R. (1988). Social work as an holistic system of activity. *Social Thought, 14* (1), 16-29.

Ingerman, S. (1991). *Soul retrieval: Mending the fragmented self.* Harper San Francisco, a division of Harper Collins Publishing NY.

Klein, W. C. & Bloom, M. (1995). Practice Wisdom. *Social Work, 40* (6), 779-807.

Krill, D. (1990). *Practice wisdom: A guide for helping professionals.* Newbury Park, CA: Sage Publications, Vol. 62.

Liebetrau, Albert M. (1983). *Measures of association,* Beverly Hills, CA: Sage Publications.

Mishlove, J. (1994). Intuition: The source of true knowing. *Noetic Sciences Review.* 29, 31-36.

Myers, I. B. (1962). *The Myers-Briggs Type indicator.* Palo Alto, CA.

Noddings, N. & Sore, P. (1984). *Awakening the inner eye: Intuition in education.* New York: Teachers College Press, Columbia University.

Noetic Science Bulletin (1994/1995).

Raines, J. C. (1990). Empathy in clinical social work. *Clinical Social Work Journal, 18* (1), 57-72.

Rew, L. (1986). Intuition: Concept analysis of a group phenomenon. *Advances in Nursing Science, 8* (2), 21-28.

Rowan, R. (1986). *The intuitive manager.* Boston: Little, Brown & Co.

Salk, J. (1983). *Anatomy of reality: Merging of intuition and reason.* New York: Columbia University Press.

Schultz, B. L. (1994). Intuition in business. *Intuition, 2* (1), 15-20, 38-40.

Simonton, O. G., Mathews-Simonton, S. & Creighton, J. (1981). *Getting well again.* New York: Bantam Books.

Sorokin. P. (1957). *Social and cultural dynamics.* Boston: Porter Sargent Publisher.

Sorokin. P. (1941). *The crisis of our age: The social and cultural outlook.* New York: Dutton.

Sullivan, D. (1992). Portrait of a prophet (Bill Kautz). *Omni, 14* (7), 40 (8).

Summers, R. (1976). *A phenomenological approach to the intuitive experience.* (Doctoral dissertation, California School of Professional Psychology, San Francisco, 1976/1977.) *Dissertation Abstractss International, 37* (8), 4171-B.

Truax, B.M. (1985). The intuitive dimension of the therapists consciousness: A new paradigm. (Doctoral dissertation, Western Michigan University, Kalamazoo, 1985/1986). *Dissertation Abstracts International, 47,* (1), 90.

Webster's third new international dictionary (1993). Springfield, MA: Miriam-Webster, Inc.

Wescott, M. R. (1968). *Toward a contemporary psychology of intuition: A historical, theoretical and empirical inquiry.* New York: Holt, Rinehart & Winston.

Wilber, K. (1993). *The Spectrum of consciousness.* Wheaton, IL: Quest.

Winter, T. (1988). *Intuitions: Seeing with the heart.* West Chester, PA: Whitford Press.

Taoism and the Strengths Perspective

Terry Lea Koenig
Richard N. Spano

SUMMARY. This article attempts to expand the contemporary strengths perspective in social work by moving beyond its reliance on Western science and philosophy. The authors suggest that Eastern philosophy may provide broader and richer underpinnings for understanding the strengths perspective. The article examines the basic tenets of the strengths perspective which include: (1) an emphasis on reality as constructed out of lived experience; (2) a redefinition of expertise in the helping relationship; (3) a challenge to expand our understanding of knowledge; and (4) a focus on supporting clients' strengths. All of these tenets are then examined in the light of the Chinese philosophical tradition of Taoism. Five themes from the Taoist tradition are explored and applied to the strengths perspective: (1) reality is a process of constant flow and change; (2) holistic dualism or the blending of two aspects into one whole; (3) nonaction or *wu wei* as a way of acting that keeps us in harmony with an ever-changing universe; (4) all-at-one-time knowledge which allows us to move from linear, abstract thinking to incorporate deeper levels of knowing drawn from ideas, instincts, intuition, hunches and the unconscious; and (5) virtue (*te*) which represents an internal power central to healing. Finally, this article identifies additional sources in

Terry Lea Koenig, LSCSW, is affiliated with the Veteran Administration Medical Center, Social Work Department, 4101 S. 4th Street, Leavenworth, KS 66048. Richard N. Spano, PhD, is Associate Dean of the University of Kansas School of Social Welfare, Twente Hall, Lawrence, KS 66045.

[Haworth co-indexing entry note]: "Taoism and the Strengths Perspective." Koenig, Terry Lea, and Richard N. Spano. Co-published simultaneously in *Social Thought* (The Haworth Pastoral Press, an imprint of The Haworth Press, Inc.) Vol. 18, No. 2, 1998, pp. 47-65; and: *Spirituality in Social Work: New Directions* (ed: Edward R. Canda) The Haworth Pastoral Press, an imprint of The Haworth Press, Inc., 1998, pp. 47-65. Single or multiple copies of this article are available for a fee from The Haworth Document Delivery Service [1-800-342-9678, 9:00 a.m. - 5:00 p.m. (EST). E-mail address: getinfo@ haworthpressinc.com].

the social work literature that may be useful in developing the strengths perspective when viewed through these Taoist themes. *[Article copies available for a fee from The Haworth Document Delivery Service: 1-800-342-9678. E-mail address: getinfo@haworthpressinc.com]*

In the past fifteen years, a small cadre of social workers began challenging the profession to examine the limitations of the dominant practice models which are rooted in a Western positivistic science tradition. This confrontation was part of a broader intellectual debate that focused on examining the role of both Western science and the role of professions in society. In social work, these writers questioned some of the following basic assumptions of Western positivistic science: (a) reality can be tested and measured in an objective manner; (b) the focus of the worker is to employ expertness to solve client problems; (c) cause and effect can be determined in some linear fashion; and (d) knowledge and values are distinguishable, with objective, quantifiable knowledge being most central to guiding practice (Blythe & Witkin, 1992; Heineman, 1981; Imbrogno & Canda, 1988; Peile, 1988; Saleebey, 1992; Weick, 1983). This article expands and augments the strengths perspective which has emerged as a product of this larger debate. The basic tenets of this emerging strengths model for practice include the following: (a) an emphasis on reality as constructed out of lived experience; (b) a redefining of the nature of expertise in the helping relationship; (c) a challenge to expand our understanding of knowledge; and (d) a focus on supporting clients' strengths. Although the strengths perspective emerged from a critique of Western scientific assumptions, it generally relies on Western intellectual sources. It is our contention that the strengths perspective can be enriched by integrating motifs found in Eastern philosophy and religion because these emphasize the importance of holistic thinking. Specifically, the Taoist mystical tradition of Chinese philosophy is used to amplify and build on the strengths perspective.

The ancient spiritual tradition called Taoism originated as a form of Chinese philosophy and religion in probably the third or fourth century B. C. E. Three major strains of Taoism developed in China: (a) those who valued mystical experience which allowed people to transcend ordinary life; (b) priests who practiced in the local communities using alchemy, magic and rituals; and (c) lay Taoists who lived in ordinary society and acted on Taoist principles (Nielson et al., 1983; Saso, 1989). We believe the following five principles taken from the mystical strain of Taoism may provide a framework for enriching our understanding of the strengths perspective: (a) reality as an unceasing process, (b) holistic dualism and its impact on our understanding of good and evil; (c) creative nonaction; (d) all-at-one-time knowledge; and (e) virtue or effective power which flows from our awareness of the Tao as the natural way and creativity of the universe.

It is important to note that a framework fraught with many words defies the spirit of Taoism. Languages by their very linear nature, spitting out one word at a time in typewriter fashion, distort the meaning and intent of Taoism. As the sage Lao Tzu said, "The Tao that can be told is not the eternal Tao" (Lao Tzu, 1988). In presenting Taoist thinking, each theme is so connected to the other themes that it is difficult to pull out only one strand. We acknowledge that this type of circular writing illustrates the Taoist respect for an all-at-one-time knowledge and holistic thinking. These ideas serve as a backdrop to our discussion of the following five crucial themes in Taoism.

REALITY AS A PROCESS

The first theme is that reality is a process of constant flow and change (Imbrogno & Canda, 1988). As water that flows in a meandering river, rushing past obstacles, and slowly, often imperceptibly changing its path with each encounter–this ever moving and ever changing water is a metaphor for the Tao. Tao literally means, the Way; in this context, it means the Way of Reality. This is similar to the idea of a Western pre-Socratic philosopher named Heraclitus. He appears to be one of the first Western thinkers to portray this ever changing reality. In fragments of his writings, T. M. Robinson (1987) expounds on a translated quote by Heraclitus which states, "As they step into the same rivers, different and (still) different waters flow upon them" (p. 17). This quote points to unity amidst change as well as universal flux and constant movement. This description of an ever changing reality is not unlike what quantum physicists more currently have been discovering about subatomic particles that are encountered in nature. Contemporary philosophical reflections stimulated by discoveries in quantum physics reflect the West's coming to terms with ancient Eastern and for our purposes, Taoist thinking. As illustrated by Capra (1982), even

> when we magnify such a "dead" piece of stone or metal, we see that it is full of activity. The closer we look at it, the more alive it appears . . . the molecular structures . . . are not rigid and motionless, but vibrate according to their temperature and in harmony with the thermal vibrations of their environment. (p. 88)

On a subatomic level, energy is constantly moving and yet at the same time maintains a dynamic balance. Not only are subatomic particles involved in a continual dance, but these particles are affected by and interact with the scientist's observations–the scientist cannot escape from forever changing the river! Subatomic particles, rivers and ultimate reality–everything is in unceasing motion.

Embedded in the strengths perspective are several notions that raise important questions regarding the nature of reality. The model's emphasis on knowledge that rests on "lived experience" and "local knowledges" places clients in a central position in the helping relationship to create meaning that has relevance to a specific person and situation, and accrues over time. This emphasis on wisdom and truth as opposed to grand theories suggests a more process oriented perspective, one less static than the traditional scientific paradigm. Further, concepts like collaboration and empowerment also appear to highlight the importance of a search or journey that creates meaning and involves both the worker and the client in the process. Reality in this model emerges from a fluid process rather than a static snapshot of a frozen world waiting to be understood by some process of laboratory analysis. Strengths oriented writers clearly value experience and wisdom over more positivistic, scientifically based approaches which they see as having inherent problems and limitations for social work. As Weick (1992, p. 23) states, there is a need for understanding human growth and development, and we would add reality itself, that is "unhinged from a lockstep view of what is considered 'normal' development to more fluid models that acknowledge creativity and powerful energy underlying all human growth."

Taoist thinking provides such a model with its broader understanding of the processes that unfold as a part of the human condition. Taoist traditions emphasize a constantly changing universe, a connection of all things to each other (holistic view), an emphasis on relinquishing effort to control others and nature, and a need to create a space for others to grow. All these insights are compatible with the approach of practitioners using a strengths perspective. In the Taoist tradition, reality is not defined by isolated superficial events, but by coming to a deep understanding of the patterns, processes and meanings of events. This is generated by trusting our inner vision. This fluid and holistic sense of reality is illustrated in a brief story attributed to Huai Nan Tzu (Mitchell, 1982, p. 126):

A poor farmer's horse ran off into the country of the barbarians. All his neighbors offered their condolences, but his father said, "How do you know that this isn't good fortune?" After a few months the horse returned with a barbarian horse of excellent stock. All his neighbors offered their congratulations, but his father said, "How do you know that this isn't a disaster?" The two horses bred, and the family became rich in fine horses. The farmer's son spent much of his time riding them; one day he fell off and broke his hipbone. All his neighbors offered the farmer their condolences, but his father said, "How do you know that this isn't good fortune?" Another year passed, and the barbarians invaded the frontier. All the able-bodied young men were conscripted and nine-tenths of them died in the war. Thus good fortune can be disaster and vice versa. Who can tell how events will be transformed?

In a dynamic, unfolding and certainly unpredictable universe, professionals would do well to be cautious about acting in ways that suggest certainty based on professional expertise related to predicting outcomes. This is compatible with the strengths perspective which places values at the heart of its practice perspective. Traditional social work values including respect, mutuality, honesty, devotion, justice, and trust are congruent with Taoist thinking and provide a context within which both the client and worker can engage in a process of mutually searching out, and exploring "reality."

HOLISTIC DUALISM AND PRACTICE

Secondly, holistic dualism, meaning the recognition of the complementarity and inter-relatedness of opposites is central to Taoism (Imbrogno & Canda, 1988). Taoism asserts that elements such as masculinity and femininity, activity and receptivity, and light and shadow are not dichotomous opposites, but represent complementary aspects of one whole. Such oppositives are understood to be reflections of the dynamic complementary polarity of two cosmic principles that interact in the flow of Tao, *yang* (activity, light) and *yin* (receptivity, shadow). Reality needs to be understood in terms of whole patterns. A pattern loses meaning and imbalance occurs if it is broken down or reduced into parts. An example in Taoist writing of the idea of holistic dualism and dynamic balance is found in the *Tao te Ching*. This book is a collection of poetry and aphorisms which sets forth the basic principles of the Tao and is attributed to Lao Tzu who traditionally is understood to have lived from 551 to 479 B. C. E. Lao Tzu writes,

As it acts in the world, the Tao is like the bending of a bow. The top is bent downward; and the bottom is bent up. It adjusts excess and deficiency so that there is perfect balance. It takes from what is too much and gives to what isn't enough. (Mitchell, 1988, p. 77)

To push the idea of holistic dualism further, it may be useful to look at an example. Two supposedly polar opposites, good and evil, are understood very differently in Taoism than they are in Western philosophy and religion. In Taoism, what is portrayed as evil is anything that is out of balance, or distorted, through emphasis on one end of a continuum over the other. In Taoist thinking, both good and evil exist side by side. By defining an act or person as only good or as only evil, we locate them on one end of the continuum. In doing so, they cease to be an ever changing reality. We render the person or act motionless when we define her or him by one of these labels. Taoist thinking portrays every element of reality as constantly changing and in a state of becoming. Maintaining a dynamic balance between any set of polar opposites is considered good. However, in much of Western philosophy and religion, if a person does something wrong, they commit a sin. In the Christian doctrine of original sin, sinning is a reflection of every person's inborn sinful nature. In this Western perspective, our human nature is rendered motionless–labeled as sinful or flawed to its core. Our human nature, because it is sinful, is at war with God, who represents everything that is good. Joseph Campbell describes listening to a Zen Buddhist philosopher, Dr. D. T. Suzuki, portray Western thought and religions in the following way. "God against man. Man against God. Man against nature. Nature against man. Nature against God. God against nature–very funny religion!" (Moyers, 1988, p. 56). From a Taoist perspective, which influenced Zen, dichotomous opposites appear very strange indeed, because they portray reality as a battle between hostile opposites. In contrast, Taoism chooses to focus on the complementarity and dynamic balance between opposites.

The strengths perspective challenges practitioners to move away from a medical disease-oriented model with its focus on dysfunction, pathology and deficits toward one that focuses on strengths, capabilities, resources and resiliency in both the client and the environment (Poertner & Ronnau, 1992; Sullivan, 1992). This shift is useful in providing a balanced view of practice and does provide a more positive stance toward shaping the direction of the work to be done by the client and the worker. In addition, it suggests a more holistic perspective that emphasizes human potential rather than solely focusing on deficits. At this point, we believe these first steps are useful, but limited. Most of the strengths writings depend on examples grounded in a Western scientific conceptualization of humans as biopsychosocial entities. For example, Norman Cousins' (1989a, 1989b) work and Weick's (1983) concerns about exploring placebo effects are both rooted within dualistic formulations of humans that fail to provide an integrated wholeness to our understanding of the human condition. Some of the emerging emphases on concepts such as empowerment, synergy, healing and holism may open the perspective to a broader range of onto-logical paradigms including those from Eastern traditions like Taoism.

The holistic dualism inherent in Taoist traditions could assist the strengths perspective to escape from the very trap it purports to avoid in its critique of the medical model. Where the medically oriented practice models focus on disease, dysfunction, deficits and limitations, the strengths oriented writers move to the opposite end of the continuum emphasizing health, functionality, opportunities and capabilities. While this is one way to redress or balance current emphases, it falls into virtu-ally the same epistemological problems. Something is either a resource or obstacle, functional or dysfunctional, healthy or unhealthy, and a strength or a need. From a Taoist, holistic perspective, clients' coping patterns, interpersonal perceptions and social environments are viewed as *both* potentially positive and negative. The seeds of health are found in unhealthy conditions and vice versa. For example, Victor Frankel's logo-therapy (Frankel, 1967), born out of his Nazi concentration camp experi-ence, demonstrates how profound meaning can rise from profound evil and suffering. In contrast, when ethnocentric, but well-meaning Christians imposed boarding schools on First Nations children, they perpetuated cultural genocide.

Perhaps two brief practice examples may help illustrate the usefulness of this holistic stance toward practice. First, in working in the area of sexual abuse we often meet young women whose inherent wisdom guided them to leave their bodies while they were being sexually abused. These experiences may be labelled as disassociative reactions based on psychiat-ric diagnostic models. Another way to view this reaction is to see it as an innately healthy response to the pain at the core of the sexual abuse experience. At the same time, this response may render a woman unable to later fully enter into a sensual experience in the context of a loving rela-tionship. The very thing that allowed her to survive the earlier experience has in it a potential to block her ability to reach her own potential in another context. Finding ways to explore, understand and honor both aspects of this adaptation is central to a healing process. A second example can be found in an individual who carries the diagnosis of bipolar disorder with repeated hospitalizations that are troublesome to both him and his family. After a period of time, the work focused on the "usefulness" of the patterns in his life. In carefully exploring what happened in each episode, the person became clear that he was making some choices even though there were biochemical issues involved. He explained his frustration with the problems psychotropic medication presented. The only time that he felt he was able to focus his mind and energy, and then exert some sense of control in his life was during the short period of time between the onset of the manic phase and the development of delusional thinking. Having clear thoughts, a sense of mastery, and energy to take control of his life, were sufficiently powerful goals, and healthy ones, to sustain what appeared to be "dysfunctional" behavior patterns. Once he articulated his needs and had them affirmed, he was able to free himself to seek new ways to achieve these goals.

In both examples, there was no assumption that the world or human beings can be separated into categories like functional/dysfunctional, good/bad, useful/not useful, strengths/needs, etc. Each component exists within the other and the search for growth represents attempts to establish a balance within individuals and between them and their environments. Change occurs when we first recognize the wisdom of current patterns as they enhance or disrupt the harmony between ourselves and our world.

Taoist understanding of holistic dualism is grounded in an even deeper insight into the monistic nature of reality: that ultimately, the Tao is an undivided oneness and transcends all dualistic conceptions, whether dichotomous or holistic. Therefore, it is mysterious and inexpressible. As the previous discussion implied, opposites can be complementary not only because they have potential to complete each other, but also because, more fundamentally, they arise from the same indivisible Tao. As Lao Tzu said,

> The nameless (Tao) was the beginning of heaven and earth; the named was the mother of the myriad creatures. . . . These two are the same, but diverge in name as they issue forth. Being the same, they are called mysteries, mystery upon mystery–The gateway of the manifold secrets.

THE PRINCIPLE OF NONACTION

A third major principle closely associated with an understanding of the Tao is called *wu wei* meaning nonaction. The *wu* means "not" or "non" and *wei* refers to "action, making, doing, striving, straining or busyness" (Watts, 1957, p. 31). Nonaction happens when we trust the cosmos or the universal rhythm–reality as unceasing motion–to do what it will do. Taoism maintains a profound trust in the intelligence or internal wisdom found in the natural body and core of each human being. This trust is extended to the cosmos. A deep trust of the power, healing capacities and goodness of human nature and of the earth rests in Taoist philosophy. Taoist nonaction does not mean passivity. For in Taoism, there is activity, but it is activity which flows like a river, in harmony with the natural course of human life and nature. Being in harmony with this ever changing life force or Tao is the essence of nonaction. This includes the ability to be in harmony with periods of crisis and disruption, so that one can flow with this into creative transformation (Imbrogno & Canda, 1988).

Finally, in the idea of *wu wei*, the doer and the deed become blended together to the point that distinguishing one from the other is artificial. This smooth activity that goes undetected can be found, for example, in the dancer whose skills, fiery passion and intense dedication and practice are blended to create a dance which flows and looks effortless. The dancer becomes the dance! As described by Mitchell (1988, p. ix), "Nothing is done because the doer has wholeheartedly vanished into the deed; the fuel has been transformed into the flame. This nothing is in fact everything." Our action becomes this kind of perfect action when it flows out of the core of who we are and is in harmony or balance with ourselves and others. Virginia Axline, who wrote about her work with a profoundly physically, emotionally and intellectually challenged child, is quoted in Brandon (1976), and represents an example of how a therapist may practice nonaction:

> I attempted to keep my comments in line with his activity, trying not to say anything that would indicate any desire on my part that he do any particular thing, but rather to communicate, understandingly and simply, recognition in line with his frame of reference. I wanted him to lead the way. I would follow. (p. 89)

Johanson and Kurtz (1991) also illustrate the idea of nonaction. For example, the primary work of nonaction occurs for therapists when they are able to create a safe physical setting, and can be a safe and trustworthy person so that the client's work of inner exploration or self-awareness can occur. The authors explain what happens when a therapist can create this kind of setting:

> It is a rare gift to find someone who can help by not being too helpful, who can facilitate without getting in the way, who can be involved without mixing up his own needs with ours, and who can be a midwife for transformation without taking credit away from the mother and child. (p. 101)

The strengths perspective does begin to address the idea of nonaction in its belief that clients are the experts in the helping relationship. Professionals take on the roles of collaborators and consultants, helping to facilitate the growth and development that is already present as potential within the client. This belief in a person's innate potential and growth runs parallel to the Taoist theme of nonaction, of trusting the clients' internal wisdom and letting them lead the way. Clients possess an intimate knowledge about the situation, which means that lived experience or personal truths as told through their story and narrative help create the sanction for work and also define the path that workers and clients need to follow together. Regenerative power and healing are strengths that every person possesses. As described by Saleebey, the worker needs to trust the clients' "intuitions, accounts, perspectives and energies" (1992, p. 8). At the very least, the client/worker relationship is based on a value that mutuality is crucial and that when possible, the client needs to lead, and certainly define the work. The idea of nonaction expands this notion of client as expert to include a spiritual awareness of the internal wisdom of human beings and of the entire cosmos. It also hints at ways in which a social worker may begin to actually practice or live out these core principles delineated in the strengths perspective. How does a social worker learn to become a safe and trustworthy person so that clients can do their own inner exploration and also live harmoniously in the community, society and world?

One means of practicing the art of midwifery and of becoming a safe and trustworthy facilitator is through the nurturing of mindfulness (Johanson & Kurtz, 1991; Watson, 1968). In order to get at our direct experience, Taoism calls for witnessing or being mindful of whatever occurs and for not forcing or making anything happen between the worker and client. Being mindful entails entering into the experience a client has without making judgments, being swayed by intense emotions, boredom or whatever is discovered. Mindfulness involves emptying the mind so that we can hear and learn from our clients. This receptivity may often take us to the place where social action is called for, but if so, it must be infused and initiated with clients' energies and purposes. This emphasis on client-driven social action may seem incongruent with a strengths perspective which calls for a *social worker* to challenge any form of oppression which may inhibit clients from developing their own human potential. However, Taoism suggests that one's "enemies are not demons, but human beings like himself. He doesn't wish them personal harm" (Mitchell, 1988, p. 31). What is called for in order to address oppression is an ability to see violators or oppressors with compassion–human beings like ourselves. If, instead, these oppressors of human rights are perceived by social work advocates as monsters, then conjuring up compassion for both worker and client will be difficult, if not impossible. Taoism invites and encourages oppressors into a journey of self-awareness. Granted there may be limits to inviting your enemy to "eat at your table"! As a last resort, confrontation and entering into conflict with oppressors can be necessary activities.

Studying and practicing this kind of nonviolent activity or nonaction may enhance a social worker's goal of operating from a strengths perspective which places clients at the center of their own growth and development. It also allows for agencies, administrators and others who at times take on adversarial roles with workers and clients, to join in this growth and development.

ALL-AT-ONE-TIME KNOWLEDGE

Another crucial theme of Taoism is all-at-one-time or unconscious knowledge (Watts, 1957, p. 23). This intuitive kind of knowledge can be contrasted with linear thinking which includes developing abstract concepts that can only be presented one-at-a-time. A metaphor for this holistic, immediate knowledge might be a painting of a family. Such a painting, which is presented all in one glance, can reflect at least a thousand words hinting at intimacy, distance or a myriad of other issues in the family relationships. Then, the family portrait can be contrasted to an essay which describes the characteristics of the same family delineating both intimate, conflictual or distant relationships. However, in attempting to write in a linear fashion about this family, we have to make some significant choices. How do we choose which relationships to focus on? How can we possibly capture the web of complex and intricate family relationships? Finally, which ideas do we consider the most significant and needing our attention in the written rendering of this family? In doing so we may miss other important components of the family. Not every aspect of complexity can be depicted! Hence, from a seemingly endless number of possibilities, we pick a few events or relationships to emphasize. Our linear knowledge and language provide us with a one-at-a-time understanding and also serve to focus our attention on a few out of a potentially endless number of possibilities. We are limited in our ability to grasp the whole picture (which can represent a thousand words all-at-one-time) of this family.

Alan W. Watts (1957) likened this unconscious knowledge to peripheral vision. Peripheral vision is less conscious and less bright than our central or focused vision. This kind of vision works best at night, and also when we are not looking directly at something. If we are staring with a sharp focus on an object directly in our gaze, this peripheral vision cannot be used to full capacity. When we relax our focus, or our grip, then this vision becomes more effective. Part of that effectiveness is due to the awareness that peripheral vision tends to be able to take in more objects or landscape within its visual field than central vision. Peripheral vision can be compared to all-at-one-time knowledge. This perspective is concerned with "understanding life directly, instead of in the abstract, linear terms of representational thinking" (Watts, 1957, p. 23).

This all-at-one-time knowledge fosters spontaneity and a respect for mystery. When we make decisions, inevitably we try to gather up all the necessary "facts" to exercise good judgment in our choices. At some point in this data-gathering process, we stop collecting information and act, making what we think are sound, rational choices. What really guides our decision-making process? Does our rational, data-collecting approach provide us with clear direction in the decision making process? Or do other factors such as our instincts, intuition or hunches weigh heavily in the decisions we make? Taoism would indicate that our decisions are quite often based on hunches, and that even when we perceive rational, thinking processes to be at the forefront, other, more immediate, unconscious and mysterious processes are mightily at work. A kind of mighty Leviathan is indeed swimming mysteriously under the surface. A respect for mystery and for spontaneity are important characteristics of this all-at-one-time knowledge. Living in harmony with the Tao includes respecting these mysterious processes of our own being and of the cosmos. Making decisions spontaneously and trusting the mind and body to know what needs to be done–all point to an internal, immediate and mysterious wisdom present in human beings and in all of reality.

In order to understand how the strengths perspective intersects with this spontaneous, mysterious, all-at-one-time knowledge in Taoism, it is important to describe major ideas about knowledge from the strengths perspective. Once these views of knowledge are highlighted, then parallels, places for expansion and different paths will be suggested. The strengths perspective challenges basic assumptions about the nature of knowledge, the role of knowledge in practice, important sources of knowledge in the practice encounter and the range of concepts that might inform practice. First, the nature of knowledge in this model is based on a "constructed perspective" that asserts there is no one truth, but many truths that must be understood in a social and individual context. This multiple-truths assertion varies from the Taoist teaching that there is a single truth called the Tao which is beyond our comprehension. The practical consequence is that Taoist insight opens the door to including multiple interpretations of events which capture some portion of truth. Thus, the positivist's notions of an objective reality that can be measured and verified still can be called into question. This assertion has powerful implications for social work. It creates the opening to move beyond current emphasis on empirically based research as the fundamental standard for accepting knowledge. It places the client in a central position to actively shape the encounter rather than depending on the worker to be the all-knowing arbitrator of the client's world. Concepts like mutuality and collaboration become central to practice in new ways. This contextual view of knowledge suggests a very different role for the worker. Professionals become the persons with responsibility to facilitate the unfolding of the client's own inherent knowledge and beliefs about the situation, collaborators who share their perspectives and advocates or mediators who assist the clients in developing and implementing courses of action that help realize their goals (Kisthardt, 1992). These are not new roles for social workers, but they are very different when they place the client rather than the professional at the center of the process of generating the knowledge that guides the process of change.

The knowledge that becomes relevant, then, is the knowledge clients and practitioners already have about themselves in any given moment. It is a tentative, immediate and constantly changing knowledge which honors intuition and flows out of direct experience in the trenches or lowlands. Schön (1983), whom the strengths perspective writers draw from, described practitioners who function in these lowlands: "They deliberately involve themselves in messy, but crucial problems and when asked to describe their methods of inquiry, they speak of experiences, trial and error, intuition and muddling through" (p. 43). Saleebey (1992) in delineating the strengths perspective, honors clients as also having access to this intuitive and often unrecognized knowledge. Taoism, too, describes a kind of unconscious knowledge which "goes on hunches," is based on spontaneity and a respect for not knowing or for mystery. By relaxing our grip and letting go of our focused vision or our narrow linear thinking, this powerful, intuitive, broad peripheral vision is given room to breathe.

Schön (1983) gave this tacit, intuitive knowledge a name, "knowing-in-action." This knowledge involves actions, judgments or recognitions which we are able to act on spontaneously without thinking ahead of time about them and without thinking about these actions while we are doing them. Although Schön does not use the descriptive word "mystery," he depicts these actions as often mysterious to the doers. Frequently, people who are practicing knowing-in-action or common sense may not even know how they learned to do the action. They also find it difficult to describe exactly what it is they know. Like a social worker who "smells" conflict or goes on a hunch that conflict is present within a family without having actually seen family members fighting, this knowledge has a mysterious and unexplainable quality to it. Taoism also honors this expanded vision or mysterious intuition which springs forth when we are able to relax and let go of our self conscious and goal driven work. Listen to the parable of a duke and his craftsman, a wheelwright, illustrated in the writings of Chuang Tzu (Watson, 1968, pp. 152-153), considered to be a major Taoist work:

> Duke Huan was in his hall reading a book. The wheelwright P'ien, who was in the yard below chiseling a wheel, laid down his mallet and chisel, stepped up into the hall, and said to Duke Huan, "This book Your Grace is reading—may I venture to ask whose words are in it?"
> "The words of the sages," said the duke.
> "Are the sages still alive?"
> "Dead long ago," said the duke.
> "In that case, what you are reading there is nothing but the chaff and dregs of the men of old!"
> "Since when does a wheelwright have permission to comment on the books I read?" said Duke Huan. "If you have some explanation, well and good. If not, it's your life!"
>
> Wheelwright P'ien said, "I look at it from the point of view of my own work. When I chisel a wheel, if the blows of the mallet are too gentle, the chisel slides and won't take hold. But if they're too hard, it bites in and won't budge. Not too gentle, not too hard—you can get it in your hand and feel it in your mind. You can't put it into words, and yet there's a knack to it somehow. I can't teach it to my son and he can't learn it from me. So I've gone along for seventy years and at my age I'm still chiseling wheels. When the men of old died they took with them the things that couldn't be handed down. So what you are reading there must be nothing but the chaff and dregs of the men of old."

Taoism values an all-at-one-time, intuitive knowledge that appears to be borne from our direct experience and reflects our connection to the Tao. As can be noted by this parable, Taoist writers often challenge conventional knowledge, pushing people to move out of the limits of written words and focused vision. Exploring and building on this kind of intuitive knowledge is an important way to expand the strengths perspective.

VIRTUE

The final central idea of Taoism to be discussed is *te*, a special kind of virtue or power. *Te* or virtue comes about when an individual has learned to practice nonaction, to let one's mind alone so that it functions spontaneously and in an all-at-one-time or holistic way. When the mind is left alone in this manner, it begins to show a certain effectiveness or power as in the healing powers of a plant. This healing power is defined as virtue. The writings of Lao Tzu suggest that every person is entrusted with this virtue. Intuitively and as part of our essential human nature, we naturally know what is appropriate for us to do, and then can act upon it. A Taoist perspective of virtue does not trust that rules and regulations, which come from a conscious or external place, will be something that people can hold on to when they face ethical dilemmas (Johanson & Kurtz, 1991). As noted by Lao Tzu (Mitchell, 1988),

> Throw away holiness and wisdom, and people will be a hundred times happier. Throw away morality and justice, and people will do the right thing. Throw away industry and profit, and there won't be any thieves. If these three aren't enough, just stay at the center of the circle, and let all things take their course. (p. 19)

Virtue is not easily developed, and it is difficult to stay at the center of the circle. Part of making one's way to the center and fostering a sense of self-awareness is described by Johanson and Kurtz (1991):

> Does this mean that to transform ourselves into paragons of virtue all we have to do is encourage a little inner awareness? No. It takes a great deal of, as opposed to just a little awareness. There are stages to negotiate, and also the quality of our communal life and relationships makes a crucial difference. (pp. 121-122)

A clinical practice example highlights the principle of virtue as an inherent quality which demands that we engage in the process of self-reflection over time. As a hospital social worker who practices quite often with elderly wives who have husbands with dementia, chronic pulmonary disease, or simply declining physical abilities that are difficult to care for, it is not unusual to work with people trying to discover the appropriate thing to do in seemingly overwhelming circumstances. In one particular instance, a husband was admitted to the hospital with end-stage chronic pulmonary disease. The wife had brought him into the hospital several times over the last few years and had always taken him home. This time she was uncertain if she could manage his health care because of increased care needs. He was so short of breath that walking and eating were difficult and he spent most of his days in bed. Their daughter was very supportive of her mom's option to place dad in a nursing home and felt that her father was very demanding of her mother. She was also concerned that her mom had continued to take care of her dad, succumbing to his demands, even at the risk of her own health. Medical staff in the hospital agreed with the daughter and encouraged the wife to seek nursing home placement.

The patient's wife was adamant about having her husband return home, and yet had gnawing doubts about her ability to care for him. In our conversations, she vacillated back and forth for weeks during his hospital-ization about an appropriate discharge plan. At times, she really wanted the social worker to tell her what decision to make. Should she take him home? Or should she listen to her daughter who was telling her that taking care of dad would be an incredible hardship and burden on her? Wasn't she being selfish if she placed him in a nursing home? Every time she would ask these questions, the worker would redirect them back to her. What did she want to do? At first she was unclear and seemed frozen, unable to make a decision. As the weeks went by, together we explored home health, hospice and homemaking services, and talked about what it would be like not to have him at home. We also discussed her husband's demanding nature and how she felt about continuing to wait on him "hand and foot." As she began to think through these issues, she seemed less ambiguous about a course of action. When the day for discharge came, she emphatically decided to take him home, fully aware of his demanding nature and of the difficulties she would have in caring for him. The next morning her husband died. She called the social worker and said that she was glad she had taken him home and could now live with herself, know-ing she had done what she could for him. This woman developed a grow-ing self-awareness about what was right for her to do. In the face of her husband's death, she had been satisfied with her decision. As depicted previously, virtue is something everyone possesses, but fostering a self-awareness that can lead to appropriate personal action is often a painstak-ing process. Given the common tendency to control events, it is difficult for many people to practice nonaction, to allow a decision to arise from within a person that is in harmony with one's authentic nature and that "fits" for them.

The strengths perspective places values at the heart of its guidance about how clients and workers develop and integrate a growing sense of self-awareness and virtue in their lives. Its value stance locates the client at the center of the awareness-building process. An emphasis on freedom, mutuality, respect, and human dignity supports the development of people's self-awareness which is the basis of virtue.

In the strengths perspective, lived experience or wisdom is valued over positivist scientifically derived knowledge. Constructed reality and local knowledge place the client in a more active stance in the practice encounter. The client becomes the central source of knowledges. Knowing the clients' personal truths is a crucial dynamic driving the empowerment and healing process. Thus, instead of the old notions of "knowledge (Western science) guided practice," we have a value guided practice where clients are the key actors in shaping the work. Taoism would push social work to consider the idea that every person has the ability to tap into their own virtue, or power. The social worker's responsibilities rest in creating a space and opportunities for individuals or communities to develop greater awareness and then respond with action out of this heightened sense of awareness or virtue. Taoism would say less about what specific values are needed in order to engage in practice and would place a much greater emphasis on spontaneity, holism and all-at-one-time knowing. Finally, the path to greater awareness or inner virtue is grounded in lived experience and space created between a worker and a client.

CONCLUSION

Current writing on the strengths perspective represents a challenge to many of the fundamental tenets of conventional deficit-focused models of social work practice. The strengths perspective questions our understanding of long held assumptions about the existing frameworks of helping derived from Western conceptions of human beings, their world and the complex web of relationships that exist between the two. This Western view of the biopsychosocial components of human existence represent *one* possible way of understanding practice. However, to further develop the strengths perspective, we may be well advised to move beyond conventional sources toward other world views.

This article suggests that Taoism provides a valuable philosophical and spiritual source for grounding and expanding our current thinking about the strengths perspective. The five Taoist principles articulated in this article provide a compatible framework for understanding the tentative beginnings put forward by strengths writers and for practitioners searching for ways to translate this perspective into practice. Further, it may be useful as a way to guide our selection of parallel streams of thought that have yet to come together. Finally, the Taoist themes in this article may help unify some of the parallel writings found in current social work literature drawn from varied sources including: (a) storytelling and narrative (Borden, 1992; Laird, 1985; Saleebey, 1994; White, 1990), (b) feminist perspectives on knowledge building (Berlin, 1976; Bricker-Jenkins & Hooyman, 1983; Collins, 1986; Davis, 1984; Nes & Iadicola, 1989; Sklar, 1985), (c) existentialist writings (Krill, 1990), and (d) transpersonal psychology (Canda, 1991; Cowley, 1993; Jung, 1934; Maslow, 1962; Smith, 1994). Perhaps the five Taoist themes in this article may provide a framework for integrating the parallel thinking and spiritual dimensions that not only the strengths perspective reflects, but that each of these substantive areas represents.

REFERENCES

Berlin, S. (1976). Better work with women clients. *Social Work, 21,* 492-497.

Blythe, B. & Witkin, S. (1992). Point/Counterpoint: Should undergraduate and graduate social work students be taught to conduct empirically-based practice? *Journal of Social Work Education,* 28(3), 260-269.

Brandon, D. (1976). *Zen in the art of helping.* New York: Arkana.

Bricker-Jenkins, M., & Hooyman, N. R. (1983). A feminist world view: Ideological themes from the feminist movement. In M. Bricker-Jenkins & N. R. Hooyman (Eds.), *Not for women only: Social work practice for a feminist future* (pp. 7-22). Silver Spring, MD: National Association of Social Workers.

Campbell, J. (1988). *The power of myth.* New York: Doubleday.

Canda, E. R. (1991). East/west philosophical synthesis in transpersonal theory. *Journal of Sociology and Social Welfare, 18*(4), 137-152.

Capra, F. (1982). *The turning point: Science, society, and the rising culture.* New York: Bantam Books.

Chuang Tzu. (1968). *The complete works of Chuang Tzu* (Watson, B., Trans.). New York: Columbia University Press. (Original work published approximately 400 BCE.)

Collins, B. G. (1986). Defining feminist social work. *Social Work, 31,* 214-219.

Cousins, N. (1989). *Anatomy of an illness.* New York: W. W. Norton.

Cousins, N. (1989). *Head first: The biology of hope.* New York: E. P. Dutton.

Cowley, A. (1993). Transpersonal social work: A theory for the 1990s. *Social Work, 38,* 527-534.

Davis, L. (1984). Why we still need a women's agenda for social work. In L. Davis (Ed.), *Building on women's strengths: A social work agenda for the twenty-first century* (pp. 1-25). Binghamton, NY: The Haworth Press, Inc.

Frankel, V. E. (1967). Group psychotherapeutic experiences in a concentration camp. In *Psychotherapy and existentialism* (pp. 95-105). New York: Simon and Schuster.

Heineman, M. B. (1981). The obsolete scientific imperative in social work research. *Social Service Review,* 55(3), 371-397.

Imbrogno, S. & Canda, E. (1988). Social work as an holistic system of activity. *Social Thought,* 14(1), 30-46.

Johanson, G., & Kurtz, R. (1991). *Grace unfolding.* New York: Bell Tower.

Jung, C. G. (1971). The transcendent function. In J. Campbell (Ed.), *The portable Jung* (pp. 273-300). New York: Viking.

Kisthardt, W. E. (1992). A strengths model of case management: The principle and functions of a helping partnership with persons with persistent mental illness. In D. Saleebey (Ed.), *The strengths perspective in social work practice* (pp. 59-83). New York: Longman.

Krill, D. F. (1990). *Practice wisdom*. Newbury Park, CA: Sage.

Maslow, A. H. (1968). *Toward a psychology of being* (2nd. Ed.). New York: Van Nostrand Reinhold.

Mitchell, S. (Trans.) (1988). *Tao te ching* (Lao Tzu). New York: Harpercollins. (Original work published approximately 400 BCE.)

Nes, J. A., & Iadicola, P. (1989). Toward a definition of social work: A comparison of liberal, radical and socialist models. *Social Work, 34,* 12-21.

Nielson, N. C. (1983). The age of the hundred philosophers: Confucius, Lao-zi and their followers. In N. C. Nielson, N. Hein, F. E. Reynolds, A L. Miller, S. E. Karff, A. C. Cochran, P. McLean (Eds.), *Religions of the world*. New York: St. Martin's Press.

Peile, C. (1988). Research paradigms in social work: From stalemate to creative synthesis. *Social Service Review, 62*(2), 1-19.

Poertner, J., & Ronnau, J. (1992). The strengths approach to children with emotional disabilities. In D. Saleebey (Ed.), *The strengths perspective in social work practice* (pp. 111-121). New York: Longman.

Robinson, T. M. (1987). *Fragments* (Heraclitus, Trans.). Toronto: University of Toronto Press. (Original work published approximately 600 BCE).

Saleebey, D. (1992). Introduction: Power in the people. In D. Saleebey (Ed.), *The strengths perspective in social work practice* (pp. 3-17). New York: Longman.

Saso, M. R. (1989). *Taoism & the rite of cosmic renewal*. Pullman, WA: Washington State University Press.

Sklar, K. K. (1985). Hull House in the 1980s: A community of women reformers. *Signs: Journal of Women in Culture and Society, 10,* 658-677.

Smith, E. D. (1994). Addressing the psychospiritual distress of death as reality: A transpersonal approach. *Social Work, 40,* 402-413.

Sullivan, W. (1992). Reconsidering the environment as a helping resource. In D. Saleebey (Ed.), *The strengths perspective in social work practice* (pp. 148-157). New York: Longman.

Tyson, K. B. (1992). A new approach to relevant scientific research for practitioners: The heuristic paradigm. *Social Work, 37*(6), 541-556.

Watts, A. W. (1957). *The way of Zen*. New York: Pantheon Books.

Weick, A. (1992). Building a strengths perspective for social work. In D. Saleebey (Ed.), *The strengths perspective in social work practice* (pp. 18-38). New York: Longman.

Weick, A. (1983). Issues in overturning a medical model of social work practice. *Social Work, 28,* 467-471.

Between Two Worlds:
The Psychospiritual Crisis
of a Dying Adolescent

Barbara Peo Early

SUMMARY. Clinical social workers are ill-prepared by education or practice experience to deal with spiritual issues, in particular those surrounding the death of a young client. This paper presents a case study of the work of a clinical social worker through the psychospiritual crisis of the dying and death of her adolescent client. The study employs extensive clinical material to trace the emergence of the client's personal metaphors as he used them to cope with stressors in his life and finally to disengage from it. It analyzes the material within the context of spiritual development and transpersonal theory in an effort to build theory in the area of clinical social work with dying adolescents. *[Article copies available for a fee from The Haworth Document Delivery Service: 1-800-342-9678. E-mail address: getinfo@ haworthpressinc. com]*

The experience of dying and the anticipation of imminent death represent a psychospiritual crisis that can occur at any age in life. Yet clinical social workers who work with children and adolescents do not expect to

Barbara Peo Early, DSW, LCSW, is Associate Professor, The National Catholic School of Social Service, The Catholic University of America, Washington, DC 20064; and Counselor at The School for Contemporary Education, 7010 Braddock Road, Annandale, VA.

[Haworth co-indexing entry note]: "Between Two Worlds: The Psychospiritual Crisis of a Dying Adolescent." Early, Barbara Peo. Co-published simultaneously in *Social Thought* (The Haworth Pastoral Press, an imprint of The Haworth Press, Inc.) Vol. 18, No. 2, 1998, pp. 67-80; and: *Spirituality in Social Work: New Directions* (ed: Edward R. Canda) The Haworth Pastoral Press, an imprint of The Haworth Press, Inc., 1998, pp. 67-80. Single or multiple copies of this article are available for a fee from The Haworth Document Delivery Service [1-800-342-9678, 9:00 a.m. - 5:00 p.m. (EST). E-mail address: getinfo@haworthpressinc.com].

have to deal with the issue of death. In fact, social workers in general are ill-prepared to help their clients with a spiritual search for meaning, despite the profession's holistic perspective on the person-in-environment. Spiritual issues have been considered controversial in social work education (Amato-VonHemert & Clark, 1994; Cowley & Derezotes, 1994; Sheridan, Wilmer, & Atcheson, 1994; & Sheridan, Bullis, Adcock, Berlin, & Miller, 1992). Although spiritual and religious issues emerge in practice, they are often avoided by the clinician in an effort to maintain professional boundaries (Canda, 1988a; Canda, 1988b; Cornett, 1992; Cowley, 1993; Joseph, 1987; & Sermabeikian, 1994). Specific objections offered to the integration of the spiritual in clinical practice include that the spiritual is unobservable, that introduction of spirituality threatens the imposition of the social worker's religious or spiritual frame of reference on the client problem, and that acceptance of spirituality confirms that there are aspects of human nature that are beyond our capacity to adapt (Cornett, 1992). Yet the spiritual is unavoidable. One respondent in Canda's (1988a) study of social workers' practice experience with spirituality remarked that, "Social workers are like sleep-walkers. They are engaged in a deeply spiritual activity, but often lack awareness of this" (p. 45).

PURPOSE

This paper will present a case study of the work of a clinical social worker through the psychospiritual crisis of the death of her adolescent client. The study traces the emergence of the client's personal metaphors as he used them to cope with stressors in his life and finally to disengage from it. It will analyze the material within the context of spiritual development and transpersonal theory in an effort to build theory in the area of clinical social work with dying adolescents.

It is important to note that the study is limited solely to the work of the author with the young man. He was also supported in his dying by his family, teachers and therapists at school, pastors, hospice nurses and a hospice social worker.

THE CLIENT

In the fall, Brent turned 18 years old. I had spent four years with him in school-based counseling. Brent attended a special education school due to the learning and emotional effects of surgery, radiation therapy, and the underlying malignant brain tumor that had been discovered when he was eight years old. He had been in remission for ten years, but just prior to his 18th birthday, the latest MRI scan indicated rapid growth of the tumor. The prognosis was death within two weeks to two months, yet Brent lived and worked a remarkable three months.

History: Understanding the Metaphors

When I first met 14-year-old Brent, he was growing rapidly, which to me seemed typical of a young adolescent. However, he pointed out that his progress was uneven and abnormal, since radiation damage to his pituitary gland required that his growth hormone and testosterone be supplied artificially. In fact, Brent usually made it a point to note that he was not growing. The first major theme that emerged in his therapy was that the doctors had told his parents that his brain had stopped growing at the time of the initial surgery when he was eight. Whatever it was that the doctors had said, Brent interpreted it to mean that his *mind* had stopped growing. It was easy to see Brent's use of this misinformation to avoid the struggle to learn new things, like two-column subtraction with borrowing. It was more difficult to recognize that attribution as a defense against the fear of the ultimate separation. Brent presented himself as Peter Pan. As it was for Peter Pan, Brent's staying a little boy, refusing to glance toward an uncertain future, was safe.

Unlike Peter Pan, who searched for a mother, Brent had one to envelop him within that safe place. Brent's loving family of father, mother and younger brother supported him well, but family and school alike wanted to help him become more independent in doing the normal everyday kid things, like not letting his mother pick out his clothes in the morning. However, if I were to explore any area around separating a bit from mother, Brent would demonstrate a defense I called "the turtle." He would shrink into his shirt, lower his eyes, become very still and silent, and leave me to observe that the turtle had retreated to his shell, and I might as well quit for the day.

Brent could also be expressive, at first through drawing and later through writing illustrated stories. The themes in his drawings and stories were consistent. He drew cities or forts under attack by multiple missiles. Often his edifices were in outer space. Brent's science fiction tales of space battles became the metaphors through which he expressed his own conflicts. He appeared to defend against three levels of "missile attack." At the most concrete level, he disliked going outside or participating in Physical Education because he was afraid of flying insects, or flying volley balls, that might hit his head, of which he was understandably protective. At a somewhat more symbolic level, Brent wanted to avoid the slings and arrows of teasing by other students. One particularly cruel incident involved a boy calling him "Radiation Man." However, at a yet deeper and even less conscious level, Brent appeared to continue to feel bombarded by his disease, by cancer cells, perhaps, or whatever he conceived to be the internal missiles attacking his fortress. Such fear of attack disturbed even his sleep. Brent would reveal that he was afraid to go to sleep at night for fear that aliens from outer space might come through his window and abduct him. In another version, aliens would inject him as he slept, as he had been injected in so many medical procedures.

Over time, and with the combined good efforts of Brent, his family, his teachers, and others who worked with him at school, he made remarkable progress toward becoming a more independent young man. He developed particular interests and expertise–paleontology and science fiction. Though he continued to hate math (pleading his poor short-term memory), he consumed science fiction novels at a remarkable pace. In spite of himself, Brent finally came to an important insight after about two years of efforts by teachers and social worker. One day Brent described some good work he had accomplished, and once again I pointed out that an eight-year-old could not do such things. Brent reluctantly agreed that his mind had indeed grown in the last few years. As time went on, he slowly began to project himself, albeit tentatively, into his future.

The Last Autumn

The first time I saw Brent in the autumn following the new diagnosis, he appeared his usual self. I admired his T-shirt, and he offered that he liked another better–one with a flaming skull on the back. I began by saying that I knew he was sick now, and I asked what he was wondering about. He came right to the point, "when it's going to kill me." I offered him a new contract. I would work with him as long as he lived. I would see him at school, once a week formally, and another day just to have lunch with him and his class. If he was too sick to be at school, I would come to his house. Though he did not have to talk about his dying, I encouraged him to do so. He said that that would be "o.k." It was my intention to try to be helpful to him in completing his life. How he approached this, through psychological, religious, or spiritual means, I said I would stick with him.

Brent did not hesitate to discuss his worries. He recalled his recent trip to the hospital. He knew now that he was going to die, but had no specific time frame. He wondered about the date and time of his death. At first he said he wanted to know; then he said that knowing would scare him. He knew he wanted to continue to be conscious enough to keep thinking, to be able to watch TV. He did not want to be kept alive by machines, but was clear that if there was any hope for a cure, he would be interested.

Brent said he wanted to finish a novel he was reading about robots fighting. I noted the similarity of that novel to his drawings and his own stories and he agreed.

I asked if there were other things he would like to do before he died. He wanted to go to a rock concert, but thought his mother would worry he would get trampled.

I asked him to tell me about the picture he had drawn. He described a typical theme–a scene with an enormous building being bombarded by small robots. Inside this building was a rather tranquil city, self-sufficient, but tenaciously defending against "pillage and looting." I wondered about the status of the battle, which he described as "a standstill." As always, I considered these scenes to be his metaphor for his own battle. The battle was currently at a standstill, but it would soon change. I was surprised at his apparent lack of anxiety, in view of the anticipated turn in the battle. I asked Brent if he were scared and he retorted, "wouldn't you be?" Despite his awareness of that fear, he was astoundingly open and willing to talk. The turtle was no longer evident.

The Dream

Within a month, Brent was no longer able to attend school. When I met with him for the first time at home, his mother ushered me into the living room, now fixed up as "Brent's room." Though it was only October, a Christmas tree lighted the corner, lego structures graced the bay window, the bird cage stood beside his chair that sat close to a hospital bed. Brent reclined in the chair, eating his breakfast. He was wearing an eye patch to avoid the double vision caused by the growing tumor. That morning he seemed slower; his words slurred more. Brent's mother used the opportunity of my being there to drive her younger son to school. After she left, Brent seemed weary and hard to engage, until out of the blue he said, "I had a dream on Saturday night."

Brent told me about his dream, "A space ship came down and picked me up and took me to heaven." Until he knew he was dying, Brent and I had not discussed heaven, afterlife, or religious issues. It appeared that the aliens who had earlier occupied a psychological space, might be better seen now in a spiritual realm, and I had agreed to discuss anything. Brent went on, "On board the spaceship, the interior looked like a movie theater, with seats and it was dark." I was wondering if he felt alone, without his usual supports, so I asked, "Were there others?" "Yes, but I couldn't see who; it was dark."

Since going outdoors had always been a terrifying experience for Brent, I inquired, "Did the ship pick you up indoors or outdoors?" "Outdoors," he replied, "I saw it land in the cul de sac and I walked out. A door opened and I climbed in. It took off. I heard someone talk in a strange language. I sat down–I had a feeling the voice had said, 'sit down.'"

Hesitantly I asked, "Were you dead?" "I couldn't feel anything, so I guess so," he replied unconcerned. When I questioned Brent how he felt about the trip, he responded with his typical disdain for discussing feelings. So I listed feelings, both positive and negative. He then decided he had felt "scared and excited."

He went on that, "A little ship took me to the mother ship, where I sat down and went off to heaven. The mother ship went into orbit, went down to heaven." Though he had left his own mother behind, the image of the ship towards which he was headed was a "mother ship," and apparently he felt quite safe.

I asked him to tell me about the feelings of scared and excited. Brent responded, "I was scared because I wasn't sure where they were taking me–hell or another planet. There were two big ships, I saw from the little one. The other big one looked like a prison ship." "But yours?" I asked. "It looked like an ordinary space ship." "Did you get to choose which ship?" "I had no decision," he replied.

I probed, "Once you got on the mother ship, did you feel any different?" "Still kind of scared," he said. Though Brent's choice was out of his hands, he saw the two possible paths. One was to the end of fear in the beckoning mother ship through disattachment to his own mother, and the other was to hell, to imprisonment, perhaps by remaining attached. I asked Brent when he knew he was in heaven, and he responded that it was when the mother ship moved into orbit. I wondered if he had still been scared then. At first he said he was, then, "Well, once I knew it was heaven, I wasn't scared anymore."

I thought the dream was over, but Brent went on to tell me the excited part, "They moved me to a 5,000 story apartment building in heaven, it was real tall. I was on the 4396th floor. Across the hall from my room, Elvis lived." I ventured some humor, "So I guess he really is dead?" Brent laughed and agreed and went on to note two more prematurely dead musicians in his building, "Kurt Cobain was on one side, and Jimi Hendrix on the other." To his rock star neighbors he added that Albert Einstein lived down the hall, explaining, "There was a list of names in the lobby, of who lived there." He proceeded with his story, but I knew I must come back to those neighbors.

Brent described his heaven, "The layout in my apartment was pretty cool. On one wall were Metallica posters. On one side was a CD player and a bunch of CD's." I reminded Brent of his earlier concern that he might not be able to take heavy metal music to heaven, since he had wondered if God might object. "I guess it isn't a problem," I quipped. "Right," he replied.

At a pause in his recounting, I decided to point out how different his dream had been from his typical behavior, so I recalled how he used to be scared to go outside at night alone, because he worried that he would be abducted by aliens, be separated from his family, particularly his mother. In Brent's dream, that is precisely what did happen, yet apparently he felt comfortable enough to venture off on his own. Once in his heaven, Brent was content to live in an apartment alone, something he had had difficulty envisioning for a future in life. I asked, "So, when you went out, where was your family?" Brent seemed puzzled but unconcerned, "I don't remember. They were kind of left out. Mom was asleep." I was surprised, "Brent, why did you walk out into that dark cul-de-sac alone at night?" He responded with remarkable calm, "I knew they were coming for me." Whoever they were, coming to separate him from the familiar, Brent no longer saw them as alien.

I returned to my puzzlement about his neighbors. I said I could under-stand why the dead rock stars were in the heaven of an 18-year-old, but wondered why he thought Albert Einstein was included. Brent responded with disgust, "I thought the atomic bomb was cool," but then he became silent. I suggested that perhaps Einstein was there because Brent had always had so much concern about his brain, and Einstein had had a wonderful brain. I reminded him how his family and those of us at school had all been surprised at how far he and his wonderful brain had come, in fact that despite many obstacles, he had completed all of his high school credits. "Yeah," Brent replied, "And I didn't flunk math." It took me a minute until I understood, "Right, Einstein flunked math didn't he?" I continued, "But his life was a success, even so." I asked Brent, "Has your life been a success?" "Yes," he replied with conviction.

Unfinished Business

Despite the comforting message of the dream, Brent had unfinished business to attend to before he was ready for his journey. Over the next two weeks, Brent related three concerns. The first was that he was worried about his mother. He was afraid, from some of the things she had said, that she might want to join him and kill herself following his death. Brent's second worry was that he thought he might not be good enough to go to heaven. He said he had asked his pastor if he were good enough for heaven, and recalled that the pastor told him "maybe" (although it seems hard to imagine that that is what the pastor intended). The last concern was Brent's questioning of his doctor's continued orders for weekly MRI's. These trips took considerable effort and wasted precious time, and Brent could not see the point. I wrote the concerns down on a piece of paper as a reminder to Brent to bring them up with his family. When I asked him what to do with the paper, he told me to post it on the refrigerator, effectively announcing them to the world, so we could deal with them openly.

THE PSYCHOSPIRITUAL CRISIS OF DEATH

Spiritual Development and Adolescence

The experience of dying, as with any life event, is affected by one's developmental stage. Erikson (1963) described the adolescent psychosocial crisis as identity vs. role confusion. During this period, youth pull away from parents to formulate an independent sense of self. If they are thwarted in doing so, perhaps by a life threatening illness, they risk a confusion of role. While all adolescents are pulled by the psychosocial task of disattaching from parents and establishing an independent identity, some are also pulled by the familiar safety of remaining attached. In a recent study, the authors (Rait, Ostroff, Smith, Cela, Tan, & Lesko, 1992) point out that normally a family with adolescents is in a centrifugal stage in which the parent-child bonds loosen. However, when an adolescent is coping with cancer, the family must and does pull closer together. This necessary closeness may inhibit the adolescent development of a survivor of pediatric cancer who can "be pulled in opposite directions: drawn to the periphery of their family as expected during adolescence and engaged in a heightened level of closeness that often emerges during the acute illness experience" (p. 386). The family's resolution of these contradictory pulls is seen as essential to adjustment of the adolescent cancer patient. Bull and Drotar (1991) found that children and adolescents with cancers in remission use coping strategies that are unique to their age and developmental stage. They tended to use intrapsychic coping mechanisms for both general and cancer-related stressors including the use of fantasy and other internal and emotion-focused coping. Also, adolescents used emotion management more than problem solving coping strategies with cancer-related stressors. Brent, too, was affected by contradictory pulls and coped through his use of fantasy to manage his emotions.

In addition to the experience of dying being affected by the life stage psychosocial crisis, that experience may also be viewed as a psychospiritual one. A psychospiritual crisis is one in which spiritual issues must be confronted in order to resolve the crisis and move on to further development. Spirituality is as much a part of the human search for fulfillment as any other aspect of humanity. Canda (1988a) views spirituality as a search for meaning that arises from an inner need. He emphasized that suffering and alienation are part of human life, so spirituality "involves confronting these courageously and faithfully while developing a sense of meaning and fulfillment that enables coping and transcendence" (p. 43).

Sermabeikian (1994) recognizes spirituality as one weapon in clients' coping arsenals, and that its use strengthens the clients' capacity to meet needs and promote mental health. She remarks,

> The spiritual perspective requires that we look at the meaning of life, that we look beyond the fears and limitations of the immediate problem with the goal of discovering something inspirational and meaningful rather than focusing on the past and on pathology. (p. 179)

Canda's (1988b) respondents agreed that for social work practice to be sensitive to the spiritual, practitioners must explore the meaning of life events with their clients, specifically in exploring the meaning in suffering, reflecting Jung's (1933) concept that human beings develop from instinctual to spiritual beings through the challenges that life brings. Brent was exploring the meaning of his struggles as he faced the challenge of the psychospiritual crisis of his dying. He was putting aside the psychosocial tasks of the instinctual being and moving towards the spiritual.

Transpersonal Theory: Moving Beyond the Ego in Adolescence

Current practice theories do not integrate the spiritual with the instinctual so that understanding and intervening with clients might help them cope with what is perhaps life's greatest challenge–the coming to terms with one's own dying. Cowley and Derezotes (1994) suggest that transpersonal theory provides the concepts to enable such integration. Within the theory, the spiritual is seen as "an essential aspect of being that is existentially subjective, transrational, nonlocal, and nontemporal" (p. 33). The authors argue that social work's avoidance of religious and spiritual aspects of the person in situation lies at the foundation of a flawed capacity to understand human behavior. Theories of psychosocial development seek self-actualization or self-fulfillment as the ultimate goal of human development. The transpersonal perspective expands the concept of self-

actualization beyond the ego, beyond time and space to spiritual fulfillment or a self-transcendence. Transpersonal development occurs,

> through the process of decentering, an evolution of consciousness
> occurs that moves individuals away from an exclusive identification
> with the ego or little self . . . thus, from the development of the
> spiritual and moral dimensions comes spiritual maturity or the
> higher states of consciousness. (p. 34)

Smith (1995) has provided a conceptual framework for the confrontation of one's mortality through transpersonal theory. To her, transpersonal
development includes the dimensions of spiritual awareness and a personal death perspective. In an earlier study, Smith, Stefanek, Joseph, Verdieck, Zabora, and Fetting (1993) found that within an interactive process
in which a comforting personal perspective on death and a heightened
spiritual awareness evolve, the psychosocial distress that adult cancer
patients experience diminished. Smith (1995) developed a practice model
for those working with adult clients confronting their mortality–the trans-
egoic model–that facilitates a normal developmental process and relieves
psychosocial distress.

However, the earlier study (Smith et al., 1993) confirmed that age
accounted for 11 percent of the variance of psychosocial distress. As
people mature, distress regarding anticipation of death decreases. But what
of the distress experienced by an adolescent facing his death? Only a
handful of participants in the study approached Brent's age. There might
well be differences for adolescents, yet developmental issues involving
spirituality and transpersonal concepts might be applied to dying young
clients to help them not simply with self-fulfillment, but with self-transcendence.

Applying Transpersonal Theory to the Psychospiritual Crisis of the Death of an Adolescent

It is likely that for an adolescent, the process of confronting mortality
may be different than for an adult, but Brent's experience reflected much
in the transegoic model (Smith, 1995). One concept is the normalization of
death. For Brent, an adolescent on the cusp of identity and role confusion,
normalization began with his loosening of the bonds of the captivity of his
dependent and not yet competent little boy role. In that role, he was the
object of his mother's caring. She cared for him, and his role was to be
cared for, to be dependent. His impending death threatened the role, and
the first of his three concerns–his fear of his mother's suicide, that she

might wish to "go with him"– was reflective of the strength of the pull to remain within it. However, if Brent were able to resolve his fears about his mother, then he could also let go of the role. Although I offered to help Brent discuss this with his mother, he did not want help at first. Later, however, he agreed, so the hospice social worker and I raised the issue with his mother who was then able to reassure Brent that she would not harm herself.

Also within the normalization of death, Brent had to move away from a closed view of death (Smith, 1995) in which he and his family had always treated death as the enemy to be guarded against, the missiles against which the fortress defended. Brent had to give up this closed view of death in order for him to move on comfortably. Brent's dream indicated that he was moving towards a more open view–an acceptance of death as another journey in life, one in which there was to be no more fear. Yet the second of Brent's concerns threatened this progress–Brent wondered if he were good enough to go to heaven.

The heaven for which Brent questioned his adequacy was a traditional one, with traditional Christian entrance requirements. Adolescents reject the familiar. Perhaps his small and normal attempts at individuation resulted in his concern that he was no longer a "good" little boy. Joseph (1987) says that at any life stage, religion may provide emotional support and hope and fill an integrative function among those who share beliefs. On the other hand, she notes, religious beliefs can sometimes lead to guilt and encourage rigid defenses. Joseph discusses the religious dimension of the passage of adolescence. She describes the preadolescent transition in which the youth begins to question the literal acceptance of beliefs, a reconceptualization seen as crucial to the adult internalization of a set of beliefs. By adolescence, the young person acquires a searching faith, expanding his or her view beyond that of family. Adolescence marks the search for meaning and identity involving a common crisis of faith in which the person may reject institutional religion. If the adolescent's faith development includes questioning of institutional religion in the midst of his search for personal meaning and identity, the once and future comfort of the family's faith may presently be absent. Thus, the images and metaphors of formal religion may be of less comfort to an adolescent in the midst of the psychospiritual crisis of dying than the exploration of his or her own metaphors for the same universal spiritual truths. In Brent's case, the Christian images of heaven may have contributed to his concern that he was not good enough. Though it would be difficult as an objective outsider to see where this young man could be considered anything other than good, Brent's holding himself to the literal religious standard might have contributed to worry and have mitigated against self-transcendence.

To resolve Brent's concern about whether he was good enough for heaven, it appeared to me that Brent's family should be involved in either recalling the pastor, or clearing up the confusion themselves. However, at the time, I wondered if it would also be appropriate in my role to offer an opinion. I did. I told Brent that if being good was how one got to heaven, I did not see what he was concerned about. I noted that in his dream, there were two ships, one a prison ship and the other a mother ship. He had said that he had no decision as to which ship was to be his. Thus, I suggested, it appeared that his dream's message was that the decision had already been made. Later, a visit was arranged with the Hospice chaplain, and she helped to further settle that issue. Brent had at his disposal, his own very adolescent and quite uninstitutional view of continued existence beyond death that involved heavy metal music, space flight, and Jurassic Park creatures. These images of afterlife he was prepared to embrace alone and unafraid, a testament to his development as an independent adolescent. For this heaven, Brent was unconcerned about being good enough.

Another concept in the transegoic model (Smith, 1995) embodies the movement from the subjective "me," the self acting in relationship, along with the objective "me," the self acted upon in relationship, and the "I" that acts independently. Becoming independent, not being in the familiar dependent relationship, had been impossible for Brent to imagine. Yet as death neared, he was able to move from a reactive to a proactive state when he acted upon the third of his concerns and contributed to the decision for no further MRI's. Brent had been legitimately baffled by the expressed necessity for the continued procedure. There did not appear to be any connection to potential change in treatment, yet the physician kept ordering MRI's. Brent did not want them anymore, but in the past had never questioned his parents' following of doctor's orders. When he let me post this on the refrigerator, his mother had already concluded that the MRI's were pointless. Yet it enabled Brent to take a proactive part in an adult decision. His dream further reflected this change as he was able to act as the "I" and follow the call to go off in the space ship, leaving behind the dependent relationship with his family in which he was the object.

Smith (1995) encourages her dying adult patients toward ego disattachment, or disidentification. This, of course, is antithetical to the task of an adolescent who is consolidating his attachment to the ego and formulating a permanent and independent identity. Yet Brent was able to disattach while incorporating others into himself. First, Brent's possessions were precious extentions of his developing ego. As he grew nearer to his death, he gave away some cherished possessions–his lego space ships to his brother, his CD's to a friend. In the end, he was able to detach from them.

Second, Brent had to incorporate human objects into his consolidating ego. Brent had aspired, in his adolescent fashion, to become a member of a rock band. So, in his heaven were rock musicians. Also included was Einstein, another learning-disabled possessor of a remarkable mind that had been slow to develop, but did. Brent incorporated these objects into his self as he disattached his self from his material things.

Perhaps most central to human spirituality is the seeking of meaning in life (Canda, 1988a; Cowley, 1993; Jung, 1933). Brent was able to express that he found meaning in his life. He had begun to recognize the enormity of his progress from the time of his initial bout with cancer, surgery, and aggressive treatment. Not only did he progress, but he acknowledged that progress. He was even able to put himself in a category with Einstein. Brent had moved from his role and meaning in life as being flawed, one to be cared for, toward one in which he had been a soldier who struggled against the missiles. Ultimately, he had won. He confirmed this when his answer to my question, "Brent, has your life been worthwhile?" was "Yes."

CONCLUSION

Thanksgiving weekend, his family with him, Brent died. The last time I saw him I had a sense that he was ready for his space journey. In the past, Brent had betrayed his anxiety by acting the turtle; yet the turtle had departed long before Brent did. His anxiety had abated and he no longer needed the shell. Nor did Brent continue to require his mother's protection. Peter Pan grew up. Through Brent's dream and his subsequent discussion of it, Brent was able to participate in a death rehearsal and complete the unfinished business that had temporarily held the ship at bay. The three concerns resolved, the possessions given away, the business finished and the rehearsal complete, Brent was able to transcend his self toward a future he envisioned. In his dream, there were no more battles, no fortresses fending off the missiles. In fact, the only negative was the "other" ship, but Brent was sure that it was not his.

Clinical social workers can enhance their work by ending their sleep walking and recognizing that clinical work is truly "a deeply spiritual activity" (Canda, 1988a, p. 45). Particularly in working with the dying, the clients' metaphors and other coping mechanisms must be seen as the spiritual tools that they are. Brent applied and adapted his metaphors to resolve the psychospiritual crisis that he faced. He was able to transcend his ego, to let it go, and then to go it alone.

REFERENCES

Amato-Von Hemert, K. & Clark, J. (1994). Point/Counterpoint: Should social work education address religious issues? *Journal of Social Work Education* 30 (1), 7-17.

Bull, B. & Drotar, D. (1991). Coping with cancer in remission: stressors and strategies reported by children and adolescents. *Journal of Pediatric Psychology* 16 (6), 767-782.

Canda, E. (1988a). Conceptualizing spirituality for social work: Insights from diverse perspectives. *Social Thought* 14 (1), 30-46.

Canda, E. (1988b). Spirituality, religious diversity, and social work practice. *Social Casework* 69 (4), 238-247.

Cornett, C. (1992). Toward a more comprehensive personology: Integrating a spiritual perspective into social work practice. *Social Work* 37 (2), 101-102.

Cowley, A. (1993). Transpersonal social work: a theory for the 1990's. *Social Work* 38 (5), 527-534.

Cowley, A. & Derezotes, D. (1994). Transpersonal psychology and social work education. *Journal of Social Work Education* 30 (1), 32-41.

Erikson, E. (1963). *Childhood and Society.* New York: Norton.

Joseph, M.V. (1987). The religious and spiritual aspects of clinical practice: a neglected dimension of social work. *Social Thought* 13 (1), 12-23.

Joseph, M.V. (1988). Religion and social work practice. *Social Casework* 69 (7), 443-452.

Jung, K. (1933). *Modern Man in Search of a Soul.* New York: Harcourt Brace.

Rait, D., Ostroff, J., Smith, K., Cella, D., Tan, C., & Lesko, L. (1992). Lives in a balance: Perceived family functioning and the psychosocial adjustment of adolescent cancer survivors. *Family Process* 31, 383-396.

Sermabeikian, P. (1994). Our clients, ourselves: The spiritual perspective and social work practice. *Social Work* 39 (2), 178-183.

Sheridan, M. Bullis, R., Adcock, C., Berlin, S., & Miller P. (1992). Practitioners' personal and professional attitudes and behaviors toward religion and spirituality: Issues for education and practice. *Journal of Social Work Education* 28 (2), 190-203.

Sheridan, M, Wilmer, C. & Atcheson, L. (1994). Inclusion of content on religion and spirituality in the social work curriculum: A study of faculty views. *Journal of Social Work Education* 30 (3), 363-376.

Smith, E., Stefanek, M., Joseph, M., Verdieck, M., Zabora, J. & Fetting, J. (1993). Spiritual awareness, personal perspective on death, and psychosocial distress among cancer patients: an initial investigation. *Journal of Psychosocial Oncology* 11 (3), 89-103.

Smith, E. (1995). Addressing the psychospiritual distress of death as reality: A transpersonal approach. *Social Work* 40 (3), 402-413.

The Relation
Between Church and State:
Issues in Social Work and the Law

Lawrence E. Ressler

SUMMARY. The article reviews the development of legal consider-ations regarding the First Amendment and religious freedom includ-ing various interpretations and key cases of the Supreme Court about relations between church and state and their implications for social services. The author argues there is a growing interest in spirituality and religion in American society. This has encouraged a social cli-mate supporting increased private sectarian involvement in social services. Therefore, the social work profession needs to develop a model of service delivery and professional guidelines which accom-modate spirituality and religion while remaining committed to the principles of the First Amendment. *[Article copies available for a fee from The Haworth Document Delivery Service: 1-800-342-9678. E-mail address: getinfo@haworthpressinc.com]*

INTRODUCTION

Many social services are provided by religiously affiliated institutions. Recent public policy changes including the Personal Responsibility and

---

Lawrence E. Ressler, ACSW, PhD, is Professor of Social Work and MSW Associate Director, Roberts Wesleyan College, 2301 Westside Drive, Rochester, NY 14624.

[Haworth co-indexing entry note]: "The Relation Between Church and State: Issues in Social Work and the Law." Ressler, Lawrence E. Co-published simultaneously in *Social Thought* (The Haworth Pastoral Press, an imprint of The Haworth Press, Inc.) Vol. 18, No. 2, 1998, pp. 81-95; and: *Spirituality in Social Work: New Directions* (ed: Edward R. Canda) The Haworth Pastoral Press, an imprint of The Haworth Press, Inc., 1998, pp. 81-95. Single or multiple copies of this article are available for a fee from The Haworth Document Delivery Service [1-800-342-9678, 9:00 a.m. - 5:00 p.m. (EST). E-mail address: getinfo@haworthpressinc.com].

Work Opportunity Act of 1996 are likely to cause an increase of religiously based social services as government programs shift into the private sector. This article examines the legal complexities and professional challenges posed by church/state relations. First, the historical development of church/state relations in social services is presented. Secondly, relevant legal issues and case decisions are reviewed. Finally implications for social work are considered.

THE COMPLEXITY OF CHURCH/STATE RELATIONS IN SOCIAL SERVICES

It is widely agreed that both social services and the social work profession in the U.S. emanated from the religious community (Niebuhr, 1932; Marty, 1980; Goldstein, 1987; Loewenberg, 1988; Midgley & Sanzenbach, 1989; Keith-Lucas, 1989; Popple, 1993). While there have been occasional articles throughout the decades that have given attention to the relationship of religion and social work (Niebuhr, 1932; Towle, 1945; Spencer, 1956; Stroup, 1962; Keith-Lucas, 1972), there has been a marked increase of interest in recent years (Loewenberg, 1988) as is evidenced by such indicators as the frequency of related articles, new professional organizations such as the Society for Spirituality and Social Work (1990), and the reintroduction of the term "spiritual" in the Council on Social Work Education's Curriculum Policy Statement (Marshall, 1991).

This trend can be seen also in the changes in the auspices and funding of social services. While there were some public funds available for social services prior to the Great Depression, largely at the state level, the New Deal began a major shift in the delivery of social services (Marty, 1980). Between 1930 and 1978 public disbursements for social services increased from $4.1 billion to $394 billion (4.5 percent to 19.3 percent of the GNP). Private expenditures during this same time increased only slightly from $1.5 billion to $4.1 billion (1.6 percent to 1.9 percent of the GNP) (Dolgoff, 1984).

The Reagan administration, which Jansson (1993) calls the catalyst for the recent conservative movement, began a concerted effort to shift delivery of social services back to the private sector. The momentum has resulted in the landmark welfare reform of 1996 which discontinued six decades of federally funded entitlement programs in favor of capped block grants to states. The reform has dramatically modified the service delivery system from a centralized federally administered system to a decentralized state system that overtly encourages an increase in the private sector.

A significant proportion of the private involvement, which is the focus of this article, are the religiously affiliated agencies. In spite of the major shift in the delivery of social services to the public sector in the past 60 years, the religious community has maintained a consistent involvement. Marty (1980) states:

> Through it all, not all members of the religious community accepted the idea of their total migration from the social service scene. The major Catholic, Protestant, Jewish, Mormon, and other religious groups remained employers and encouragers of social workers. They did not so much abandon the field as see it diminish comparatively, especially after the great increase of government services on terms that ruled them out after the New Deal. And bearers of the Western religious traditions continued to wrestle with the issues of social service that they were not only as secular but also as somehow religious. (p. 477)

In 1980, for example, it was estimated that 47% of the private social service expenditures were associated with religiously affiliated agencies (U.S. Bureau of the Census, 1981). The recent public policy shift of social services toward the private sector will probably increase the role of religious agencies in social work.

Inherent in religious involvement in social services is a troublesome legal issue which has received little attention in the social work literature, i.e., the church/state relationship. Although the tension in church/state relations has been acknowledged occasionally (Spencer, 1956; Loewenberg, 1988; Buhner, 1992; Bullis, 1996), the issue has remained largely unaddressed. It appears that the social welfare system and the social work profession which has operated largely in a secular context for most of the 20th century will need to adjust to a more religiously oriented environment in the future. Accordingly, it is important to examine these church/state relationship issues.

One of the fundamental sources of tension regarding the relationship of religion and social services is the wording of the religious freedom portion of the First Amendment to the Constitution which reads, "Congress shall make no law respecting an establishment of religion, or prohibiting the free exercise thereof." A recent controversy regarding the Salvation Army in Carlisle, Pennsylvania, will help to illustrate the problem.

The Salvation Army, founded by William and Catherine Booth in 1865, is a Christian church with a commitment to providing social services. It now has 9,686 centers of operation worldwide. As a social service agency, the Salvation Army is one of the most popular charities, collecting over $726 million dollars in 1992 (Winston, 1994). It received an additional

$178 million dollars from the federal, state, and local governments for a variety of services (Salvation Army Headquarters personal communication, December 20, 1994).

In 1995, the Carlisle Salvation Army applied for $250,000 from a Block Grant to rehabilitate a building for transitional housing. This request was rejected by Housing and Urban Development which concluded, based on a 1986 HUD ruling, that this would be granting money to a church, thus violating the First Amendment. The provisions of the ruling, when first published in 1986, entirely precluded the use of grant funds "to renovate, rehabilitate, or convert buildings owned by primarily religious organizations or entities" (Office of Asst. Secy. for Comm. Planning, 1986). The 1986 ruling received considerable negative reaction with some arguing that "the provision goes beyond constitutional requirements regarding the separation of Church and State and would work to prevent the participation by many religious organizations" (p. 4). The provisions were subsequently modified to permit HUD grants to religiously affiliated social services if the religious organizations would create a separate secular, nonprofit organization and if the building would be used exclusively for secular purposes available to all persons regardless of religion. The Carlisle Salvation Army was fighting the requirement that it form a separate, nonprofit organization stating that it was unnecessary. Interestingly, at the same time the Salvation Army was denied the HUD grant, it was granted $18,000 from a federally funded Emergency Shelter program, a grant they receive annually.

LEGAL ISSUES AND COURT CASES

The church/state issue is likely to become more complicated in the social services for several reasons. First, the mood of government at all levels is to rely more on private organizations including religiously affiliated agencies. A recent city government plan in Washington, D.C. illustrates this trend. In response to a serious financial crisis, the comprehensive plan of Washington, D.C.'s City Council proposes to use churches throughout the city to feed the homeless, provide day care for children, and house counseling centers for drug addicts (Woodlee, 1994). The state of Mississippi provides another example. The Governor of Mississippi, as part of his welfare agenda, has begun a program called "Faith and Families" in which churches and synagogues are being solicited to be partners with the Mississippi Department of Human Services to help families move off welfare and into the work force (Mississippi Department of Human

Services, 1995). With passing of the Personal Responsibility and Work Opportunity Act of 1996, this trend will increase even more in the future.

A second reason for the increased complexity in church/state relations is the popular belief that many of the social problems in the United States are related to a spiritual and moral malaise. A *Newsweek* poll found that 76% of the adults agree that "the United States is in moral and spiritual decline" (Fineman, 1994, p. 31). In response, religious organizations are being turned to for solutions. The *Detroit News*, for example, ran numerous stories in 1994 highlighting religiously affiliated programs that are infusing social services with the goal of encouraging religious commitment. A program entitled "What's Up Ministries" was described as attempting to reduce violence by sharing the Christian faith through concerts and attracting kids to sports events (Gauch, 1994). One of the highlighted programs was Teen Challenge which uses a Bible Boot Camp to rehabilitate drug addicts (Esparza, 1994). Another program, WORD-UP Youth Outreach, was described as attempting to rehabilitate gang members using what founder Clint Kirkwood, Jr., a Detroit police officer, called "spiritual behavior modification" (Kirkwood, 1994). One community organizer describes her response to the drug problem in one particular neighborhood as "religious intervention" (Edwards, 1994). Similar reports can be found in other cities including Houston which had a news report championing as a national model, a religiously based coalition that had a 500-student child development center and a federally funded job-placement center (Brunsman, 1995). The Family Research Council (1995) is advocating a "faith based alternative to the welfare state."

SUPREME COURT CASES RELATED TO RELIGION AND SOCIAL SERVICES

The Constitution Law edition of *American Jurisprudence* (1979), a comprehensive summary of legal decisions, devoted two sections to the topic under the headings: "Aid to churches, generally"; and "Aid to hospitals or other charitable institutions operated by religious groups." With respect to aid to churches, funds and property were given directly to churches prior to the Constitution and First Amendment and for some time after as well. This pattern has been discontinued with all state constitutions now specifically prohibiting such assistance. In addition, the Supreme Court specifically ruled that taxing and spending in aid of religion were a violation of the First Amendment (Moose Lodge No. 107 v. Irvis, 1965).

But what of public funds given for social services offered by religious institutions? *American Jurisprudence* suggests, "There is very little judicial authority on whether public funds can be given to welfare institutions operated by religious institutions" (p. 294). Legal decisions on this question have been made at the state level and are somewhat inconsistent. For example, financial aid to hospitals for the care of the poor has been found to be constitutional in a number of states "as long as the hospitals served all regardless of creed and there was no effort made to advance the particular religion" (p. 293). On the other hand, several states have constitutions which ban public aid to sectarian and denominational institutions and the state supreme courts have invalidated public aid to such hospitals.

A number of state court cases have upheld the constitutionality of public support to religiously affiliated institutions which had custody of orphans and children committed by juvenile courts. Some religiously affiliated institutions were denied public support, however, particularly if they involved "religious training in the faith of the sponsoring institution" (p. 295). A decision in Nebraska (United Community Services v. Omaha Nat. Bank, 1956) "refused to allow a public body to contribute to the local community chest since this charity passed on some of the funds to religious organizations doing charity work" (p. 295). Louisiana's constitution bans aid by the state but permits local governments to support charitable and benevolent institutions (p. 295).

The Development of the First Amendment

The church/state tension is not a recent phenomenon. The issue has been the source of contention since the founding of this country. One might assume that since religious freedom is the subject of the first of the Bill of Rights, there was broad support among the founders for what Jefferson later referred to as a wall of separation between church and state. On the contrary, Gaustad (1993) demonstrated that there was an intense struggle over this issue in the years leading up to 1791 when the First Amendment was passed. He pointed out that some state constitutions developed during this same period did, in fact, develop a church/state alliance. The state of Delaware in 1776, for example, required that government officials make the following declaration "I, _____, do profess faith in God the Father, and in Jesus Christ His Only Son, and in the Holy Ghost, on God, blessed for evermore; and I do acknowledge the holy scriptures of the Old and New Testament to be given by divine inspiration" (p. 114). Georgia in 1777 and South Carolina in 1778 required that government officials be Protestants. Kentucky, New York, North Carolina, and Tennessee, on the other hand, prohibited clergy from being a part of the legislature. It was only after much deliberation and numerous drafts that the current amendment was approved. While the amendment was ratified, not everyone was pleased. Gaustad (1993) reported that one opponent from New Hampshire opposed the amendment on the grounds that, "a Turk, a Jew, a Roman Catholic, and what is worse than all, a Universalist, may be President of the United States" (p. 113).

The disagreement about the relationship between government and religion continues unabated, complicated even more by differences of opinion about the original intent of the framers of the Constitution. The Establishment Clause was interpreted by Cord (1982), for example, as intending to keep the government from authorizing a national religion while permitting nonpreferential support of religion. Levy (1986) held that the Establishment Clause was intended to strictly separate government and religion to maintain peace in a pluralistic society. Carter (1993), argued that the phrase, "no law respecting the establishment" was actually intended to protect the states rights to establish a religion if they wanted. The only certain conclusion one can make about the First Amendment is that some type of separation between government and religion was agreed to and that religious freedom was important to the framers of the Constitution. The proper balance between religion and government was as unclear and controversial then, as now.

Recent Church/State Controversies

In light of the paucity of Supreme Court cases dealing with social services and religion, it is necessary to examine church/state decisions in other arenas. With the exception of the U.S. Supreme Court decision in 1879 to uphold the bigamy conviction of George Reynolds, the secretary to Brigham Young (Reynolds v. United States, 1879), the U.S. Supreme Court was not significantly involved in church/state issues until Cantwell v. Connecticut (1940). Three Jehovah's Witnesses were found guilty of disturbing the peace for approaching people in a public setting to talk about their faith even though it was done non-coercively. The Supreme Court accepted the case arguing that the Fourteenth Amendment statement that "No State shall make or enforce any law which shall abridge the privileges or immunities of citizens of the United States" included the First Amendment prohibition against establishing religion or prohibiting the free exercise of it. According to Eastland (1993), Cantwell was the first time the Supreme Court applied the Fourteenth Amendment to the free exercise of religion and the first time that "the Court invalidated the action of a state for this reason" (p. 15).

The U.S. Supreme Court has addressed church/state issues frequently since then with educational issues receiving much of the attention. The first such case was Everson v. Board of Education (1947) which dealt with the public funding of student transportation to sectarian schools. This case was important for a number of reasons. According to Eastland (1993), this was the Supreme Court's "first significant effort to interpret the establishment clause" (p. 59). The Everson case is significant in addition because of the church/state philosophy articulated by Justice Black. In his comments for the majority, Justice Black stated, "The First Amendment has erected a wall between church and state. That wall must be high and impregnable. We could not approve the slightest breach" (Eastland, 1993, p. 67). Ironically, the majority of the justices, in a split decision, supported the practice of public funding of transportation to sectarian schools arguing that it did not breach the wall.

A year after Everson v. Board of Education, in McCollum v. Board of Education (1948) the Supreme Court agreed with avowed atheist Vashti McCollum that offering religious instruction in public school violated the Establishment Clause, even though participation was voluntary and a number of religions were included. The state of Illinois argued that the releasing of students for religious instruction was constitutional since no one religion was preferred. Justice Black, writing for the majority, disagreed, again referring to the need to keep the wall of separation high and impregnable.

The church/state issue became especially contentious with the Court's 1962 decision in Engel v. Vitale (1962). The case involved a prayer approved by New York Board of Regents for daily use in public school. The prayer read simply, "Almighty God, we acknowledge our dependence upon Thee, and we beg Thy blessings upon us, our parents, our teachers and our Country." Participation was voluntary. The Supreme Court ruled against the prayer stating, "it is no part of the business of government to compose official prayers for any group of the American people to recite as a part of a religious program carried on by the government" (Eastland, 1993, p. 421).

The "high and impregnable" standard was refined in 1971 by what came to be known as the Lemon test. The term stems from the Lemon v. Kurtzman case (1971) which dealt with the constitutionality of two state educational programs in Pennsylvania and Rhode Island. These states reimbursed private schools, including religious schools, for textbooks, materials, and the salaries of teachers teaching non-religious subjects. The U.S. Supreme Court concluded that the programs were unconstitutional. Justice Burger, in an opinion written for the majority, identified three criteria which laws must pass to be deemed constitutional with respect to religion and government. First, the law must have a secular purpose. Second, the law must neither advance nor inhibit religion. Third, the administration of the law must avoid excessive governmental entanglement with religion.

HUD's decision not to grant money to "pervasively sectarian" organizations, described earlier in the Salvation Army controversy, was based on the Lemon principles. The HUD officials concluded that such action would violate the second and third tenets of the Lemon test, that is, religion would be advanced and there would be excessive entanglement. HUD's solution was first of all to require the establishment of a separate secular nonprofit organization. Secondly, they required the assurance that the building would be used exclusively for secular purposes. Finally, they required that the services would be available to all persons regardless of religion.

There seems to be an indecisiveness about how "high and impregnable" the wall ought to be and disenchantment about the Lemon test as the device to decide church/state cases. Justice O'Connor explicitly questioned its usefulness (Lynch v. Donnelly, 1984) leading some to predict a new set of guidelines would be adopted. One such indication that a change may be occurring is the 1995 case, Rosenberger v. Rector and Visitors of University of Virginia. The case involved a Christian organization which published a student newspaper at the University of Virginia and requested funding from the student activity fee. Funds were given to 118 organizations including a Muslim Student Association and a Jewish Law Student Association. The University denied funds to the newspaper because of the religious nature of the organization which stated in its purpose, "To challenge Christians to live in word and deed, according to the faith they proclaim, and to consider what a personal relationship with Jesus Christ means" (Jaschik, 1995, p. A24). The Supreme Court ruled against the University of Virginia arguing that public colleges may not deny funds to student organizations on the basis of their religious purpose. Jaschik (1995) states about the case, "The 5-4 decision set new looser standards for the separation of church and state in public higher education" (p. A24).

While much of the church/state debate in the past 30 years has centered around the limits of government with respect to the establishment clause, there are two notable cases that have dealt with the free exercise of religion. The first of the cases, Employment Division v. Smith (1990) involved two Native Americans who were denied unemployment compensation because they had been fired for violating Oregon's controlled substance law. They had used peyote for sacramental purposes during a ceremony of the Native American Church. Smith and Black challenged the unemployment decision arguing that the use of peyote was protected under the free exercise clause of the First Amendment. The U.S. Supreme Court decided against Smith and Black and upheld the denial of unemployment compensation. The justification used by Justice Scalia, who wrote for the majority, is noteworthy. He stated,

The government's ability to enforce generally applicable prohibitions of socially harmful conduct, like its ability to carry out other aspects of public policy, cannot depend on measuring the effects of a governmental action on a religious objector's spiritual development. To make an individual's obligation to obey such a law contingent upon the law's coincidence with his religious beliefs, except where the State's interest is "compelling"–permitting him, by virtue of his beliefs, 'to become a law unto himself,' ... contradicts both constitutional tradition and common sense. (p. 872)

This decision abandoned guidelines the Court had followed since 1963 (Sherbert v. Verner, 1963) which were designed to protect the free exercise of religion from government intrusion. The guidelines permitted restrictions to the exercise of religion only if the government could prove a compelling government interest and if the restriction was the least restrictive means possible to achieve the objective. As Bullis (1996) pointed out, "This strict scrutiny made it much more difficult for government interference of intrusion into spiritual practices. The *Smith* decision short-circuited this scrutiny. The holding required only that the law be neutral for it to stand" (p. 82).

The Employment Division v. Smith decision was received with almost universal concern in the religious community and among those committed to civil rights, including the American Civil Liberties Union. There was a broad consensus that free exercise of religion was in great jeopardy. As a result, Congress passed the Religious Freedom Restoration Act in 1993 which stated that "governments should not substantially burden religious exercise without compelling justification." While the constitutionality of the law has not been tested, it nevertheless sent a message to the Court that free exercise of religion is a cherished right and should be protected unless there is a compelling reason to obstruct such behavior.

The second case, Church of the Lukumi Babalu Aye v. City of Hialeah (1993), tested the limits of free exercise of religion with respect to animal sacrifice. The city of Hialeah, Florida, passed four city ordinances banning ritual sacrifice of animals. The ordinances were developed in response to the Santeria church, an Afro-Cuban religion, that practiced ritual killing of animals as a central part of their religious ceremonies. The city of Hialeah developed the ordinances ostensibly to protect the public and to prevent cruelty to animals. The Court, in a unanimous vote, struck down the ordinances arguing that they unconstitutionally limited religious exercise. The case seemingly indicates a return to the compelling government interest standard.

Church/State Relationship Models

Over the years, the Supreme Court has articulated a number of different positions relative to the First Amendment, with some positions favoring the non-establishment clause, some favoring the free exercise clause, and some trying to achieve a balance between the two clauses. Table 1 summarizes six different approaches that Justices have endorsed in the 20th century (Lee, 1986). The opinions written by Felix Frankfurter and Hugo Black are labeled as Secular Regulation Rule and Absolute Separation, respectively. These Justices, according to Lee, demonstrated more concern

---

TABLE 1. Models of Church/State Relationship Promoted by the Supreme Court

Model of Supreme Court Justice	Summary	Legal Cases
1. **The Secular Regulation Rule–** Felix Frankfurter Anthony Scalia	Free exercise refers only to belief. Behavior is subject to government regulation.	W. Va. Board of Education v. Barnette (1943) Employment Division v. Smith (1990)
2. **Absolute Separation–** Hugo L. Black	The wall between church and state must be "high and impregnable."	Everson v. Board of Education (1947)
3. **Compelling State Interest–** William Brennan	State may not restrict religious exercise unless there is a compelling reason.	Sherbert v. Verner (1963) Walz v. Tax Commission (1970)
4. **Balancing Free Exercise Claims** (Lemon Test)– Warren Burger, William Rehnquist	Statute must have a secular purpose. It cannot advance or inhibit religion. It should not result in excessive entanglement.	Wisconsin v. Yoder (1972) United States v. Lee (1982) Bob Jones University v. United States (1983)
5. **Accommodationism–** William O. Douglas	The government can accommodate religion. It may not, however, express a preference for any one religion.	Zorach v. Clauson (1952)
6. **No Coercion–** Potter Stewart	Religious freedom must be respected. Individuals may not be coerced.	Abington Township v. Schempp (1963) Meek v. Pittenger (1975)

Based on Lee (1986)

about ensuring the non-establishment of religion than about the free exercise of religion. At the other extreme is Potter Stewart who, according to Lee, placed more emphasis on protecting free exercise rights than on ensuring non-establishment, believing that the government's primary responsibility is to guarantee free exercise and maintain a non-preferential stance to any one religion. Justices who attempted to remain sensitive to both, according to Lee, included Brennan, Burger/Rehnquist, and Douglas in positions labeled Compelling State Interest, Balancing Free Exercise Claims, and Accommodationism respectively.

Carter (1993), in his popularly received book *The Culture of Disbelief: How American Law and Politics Trivialize Religious Devotion*, argued that, overall, the rulings of the Supreme Court have been insufficiently supportive of the free exercise of religion. Carter believed that religion makes a significant contribution to a democratic society; he calls for a church/state relationship that is more accommodating to religion.

IMPLICATIONS FOR SOCIAL WORK

Carter's analysis of the relationship between law, politics, and religion is a fitting analysis of the relationship between social work and religion. Whether by philosophical intent or as a consequence of the "high and impregnable" interpretation of the First Amendment, the profession of social work and the social service delivery system have tended to trivialize spiritual and religious devotion. With the shift at both the micro and macro levels in the United States to a more affirmative view of spirituality and religion, the social work profession needs to develop a more religiously accommodating model of helping.

First, the profession must become more accommodating in its direct practice. It needs to address spirituality and religion regarding both dysfunctional aspects and the benefits that they bring to many people. This would involve teaching social workers to include spiritual and religious assessments from a practice perspective incorporating empowerment and strengths. It would also involve teaching social workers spiritually and religiously sensitive interventions. More professional wisdom and guidelines need to be developed about such topics as when it may be appropriate to pray, when to use religious language, when to bring up religious and spiritual issues, how to provide spiritual counseling and avoid spiritual abuse, when to refer to a colleague with expertise in a spiritual and religious area, and how to handle value and ethical dilemmas between family members, clients, social workers, and the agency.

Secondly, social service models need to be developed which are more accommodating to religiously affiliated organizations, including organizations which have spiritual commitment and growth among their objectives. Guidelines need to be developed concerning the provision of funding to religious organizations in a manner which utilizes their contributions, honors the self-determination of the clients, and remains committed to serving a diverse society.

Thirdly, social policy debate and formation should address the issues raised by religious involvement in social services. Social workers involved in social policy development need to become well informed about the legal issues in order to advocate for policies that protect the freedom to practice religion while also preventing inappropriate prosyletization in state funded social services.

While the First Amendment is clear that the government may not make laws establishing a religion, it also must protect the right of persons who choose to practice religion. A wall of separation between church and state is important, but as Carter (1993) indicates, "it must be one with a few doors in it" (p. 109). Surely there are professional dangers and legal restraints with respect to being more accommodating to religion and spirituality, but there are professional inconsistencies and legal problems involved in ignoring religion and spirituality, as well. Although taking a more accommodating position with respect to spirituality and religion brings uncertainties, it is far better for the profession to help shape the direction of things to come than to remain silent.

REFERENCES

American jurisprudence: A modern comprehensive text statement of American law. [2nd ed vol 16A]. (1979).

Brunsman, S. (1995, 7/January). Coalition serves The Woodlands' well-to-do, needy. *Houston Post*, pp. E, 2:1.

Buhner, S. (1992, Winter). Controversies in the regulation of spiritually oriented helping. *Spirituality and Social Work Journal*, 3(1), 18-23.

Bullis, R. (1996). *Spirituality in social work practice.* Washington, DC: Taylor and Frances.

Cantwell v. Connecticut. (1940). *U.S., 310*, 296.

Carter, S. (1993). *The culture of disbelief: How American law and politics trivialize religious devotion.* New York: Basic Books.

Church of the Lukumi Babalu Aye v. City of Hialeah. (1993). 113, S. Ct., 2217.

Cord, R. (1982). *Separation of church and state: Historical fact and current fiction.* New York: Lambeth Press.

Dolgoff, R. &., Feldstein. (1984). *Understanding social welfare.* New York: Longman.

Edwards, M. (1994, 25 September). I'm trying to deal with drugs in a city neighborhood but I've got lots of competition. *Detroit News*, pp. B, 3:1.

Employment Division v. Smith. (1990). *U.S., 494*, 872 (Supreme Court; church/State).

Engel v. Vitale. (1962). *U.S., 370*, 421.

Esparza, S. (1994, 8/September). Teens take hard road to curb booze, drub habits. *Detroit News*, pp. B:3.

Everson v. Board of Education. (1947). *U.S., 330*, 18.

Family Research Council. (1995). *The greatest of these is love: A faith-based alternative to the welfare state.* 700 Thirteenth St., NW, Suite 500, Washington, DC, 20005.

Fineman, H. (1994, 13/June). Virtuecrats. *Newsweek*, pp. 31-36.

Gauch, S. (1994, 23/August). Ypsilanti group seeks to halt the violence and save souls. *Detroit News*, pp. B, 3:1.

Gaustad, E. (1993). *Neither king nor prelate: Religion and the new nation, 1776-1826.* Grand Rapids, MI: Wm. B. Eerdmans.

Goldstein, H. (1987, May-June). The neglected moral link in social work practice. *Social work, 32*(3), 181-186.

Jansson, B. (1993). *The reluctant welfare state: A history of social welfare policies.* Pacific Grove, CA: Brooks/Cole.

Jaschik, S. (1995, 7/July). High court bars University of Virginia from denying funds to religious newspaper. *The Chronicle of Higher Education*, pp. A24-A33.

Keith-Lucas, A. (1972). *Giving and taking help.* Chapel Hill, NC: University of North Carolina Press.

Keith-Lucas, A. (1989). *The poor you have with you always.* St. Davids, PA: NACSW.

Kirkwood, C. (1994, 19/July). Giving troubled kids a lift. *Detroit News and Free Press*, pp. C: 3.

Lee, F. (1986). *Wall of controversy: Church-state conflict in America.* Malabar, FL: Robert Kreiger.

Lemon v. Kurtzman. (1971). *U.S., 403*, 602.

Levy, L. (1986). *The establishment clause: Religion and the first amendment.* New York: Macmillan.

Loewenberg, F. (1988). *Religion and social work practice in contemporary American Society.* New York, NY: Columbia University Press.

Lynch v. Donnelly. (1984). *U.S., 465*, 668.

Marshall, J. (1991). The spiritual dimension in social work education. *Spirituality and Social Work Communicator, 2*(1), 12-14.

Marty, M. (1980). Social service: Godly and godless. *Social Service Review, 54*(4), 463-481.

McCollum v. Board of Education. (1948). *U.S., 333*, 203.

Midgley, J., & Sanzenbach, P. (1989, October). Social work, religion, and the global challenge of fundamentalism. *International Social Work, 32*(4), 273-287.

Mississippi Department of Human Services. (1995). Faith and families: The governor's welfare agenda (p. 9). Mississippi.

Moose Lodge No. 107 v. Irvis. (1965). *S Ct, 92*.

Niebuhr, R. (1932). *The contribution of religion to social work*. New York, NY: Columbia University Press.

Office of Asst. Secy. for Comm. Planning, D., HUD. (1986). *Emergency Shelter Grants Program: Homeless Housing act of 1986* [24 CFR] (574.60-575.63). Washington, DC: Housing and Urban Development Committee.

Popple, P. &., Leighninger. (1993). *Social work, social welfare, and American society*. Boston: Allyn and Bacon.

Religious Freedom Restoration Act of 1993. (1993). U.S. 103rd Congress.

Reynolds v. United States. (1879). *U.S., 98*, 145.

Sherbert v. Verner. (1963). *U.S., 374*, 398.

Society for Spirituality and Social Work [A free standing group which developed in the late 1980s currently under the leadership of Robin Russel at the University of Nebraska]. (1990).

Spencer, S. (1956, July). Religion and Social Work. *Social Work, 1*(3), 19-26.

Stroup, H. (1962, April). The common predicament of religion and social work. *Social Work, 7*(2), 89-93.

Towle, C. (1945). *Common human needs*. New York, NY: NASW.

U.S. Bureau of the Census. (1981). Private philanthropy funds, by source and allocation: 1960-1980. In R. Dolgoff & D. Feldstein. (Ed.), *Understanding social welfare* (p. 238). New York, NY: Longman.

United Community Services v. Omaha Nat. Bank. (1956). *N.W. 2d*, 77, 576. Omaha.

Winston, D. (1994, 18/May). Charitable Army's goal: Emphasis on salvation. *Atlanta Journal Constitution*, p. E6.

Woodlee, Y. (1994, 18/May). Council backs feeding of poor in churches. *Washington Post*, pp. D1, D5.

Afterword:
Linking Spirituality and Social Work:
Five Themes for Innovation

Edward R. Canda

SUMMARY. This article suggests five themes to guide continued innovation in professional efforts to link spirituality with social work in a manner that is consistent with commonly held professional commitments. First, the mission to promote human fulfillment needs to be expanded to include the concepts of mutual benefit, transpersonal self-realization, and well-being for all. Second, professional concern with human diversity needs to embrace spiritual diversity and its implications for transcultural understanding. Third, the value of self-determination should take into account a transpersonal understanding of the self, including the rights of religious and spiritual groups' self-determination and the complementarity of freedom and responsibility. Fourth, theory and conceptual frameworks for social work practice need to address a truly holistic view of the person-in-environment, including transpersonal and deep ecological perspectives. Finally, the helping relationship itself needs to be revisioned in terms of spiritual sensitivity. *[Article copies available for a fee from The Haworth Document Delivery Service: 1-800-342-9678. E-mail address: getinfo@haworthpressinc.com]*

INTRODUCTION

The previous articles in this volume have demonstrated that interest is burgeoning about the linkage between spirituality and social work, among

Edward R. Canda, PhD, is Associate Professor, School of Social Welfare, The University of Kansas, Lawrence, KS 66045.

[Haworth co-indexing entry note]: "Afterword: Linking Spirituality and Social Work: Five Themes for Innovation." Canda, Edward R. Co-published simultaneously in *Social Thought* (The Haworth Pastoral Press, an imprint of The Haworth Press, Inc.) Vol. 18, No. 2, 1998, pp. 97-106; and: *Spirituality in Social Work: New Directions* (ed: Edward R. Canda) The Haworth Pastoral Press, an imprint of The Haworth Press, Inc., 1998, pp. 97-106. Single or multiple copies of this article are available for a fee from The Haworth Document Delivery Service [1-800-342-9678, 9:00 a.m. - 5:00 p.m. (EST). E-mail address: getinfo@haworthpressinc.com].

97

both practitioners and scholars. This recent rapprochement with spirituality has the potential to catalyze profound transformations in the conceptualization and practice of social work. This essay will suggest five themes that could guide future innovations in spirituality and social work. These themes were derived by considering issues raised in the preceding articles in light of frequently espoused professional commitments. These commitments are: to promote maximum fulfillment of individuals and communities; to respect and appreciate human diversity; to uphold client self-determination; to develop holistic person-in-environment understandings; and to engage in a sensitive and empathic professional helping relationship. The ideas are intended to be provocative and challenging to conventional assumptions about social work in order to encourage further debate and dialogue at this time of expanding professional interest in spirituality.

HUMAN FULFILLMENT

Social work promotes the fulfillment of individuals and communities. When fulfillment is understood in a spiritual context, the vastness of human potential is revealed. There are two directions a person can turn effort in actualizing potential. One direction is inward, following a course of introspection and self-understanding until the true nature of the self is revealed. The other direction is outward, following a course of exploring social relationships and the world until the true nature of the universe is revealed. When these directions are followed to their conclusion, they meet with each other in a full circle that embraces both self and other in mutual benefit.

Transpersonal psychology has explored the inward course of development extensively (e.g., Wilber, 1995). In general, transpersonal theory suggests that personal development can go beyond the fulfillment of ego-based identity needs and strengths to trans-egoic capacities for intuition, creativity, holistic ways of thinking, and states of consciousness in which self and world are experienced in interrelationship and unity. As Carroll discussed, spiritual development can yield deep insights into the meaning and significance of one's life and an integration of all aspects of oneself. Early's case study was a poignant account of terminal illness as a catalyst for spiritual development. Through spiritual development, a person grows in a sense of integrity in a profoundly literal sense; that is, physical, intellectual, emotional, and intuitive aspects of the whole self are integrated and function more harmoniously. Luoma and Koenig and Spano discuss this intuitive, spontaneous, and harmonious way of being. As they point out, achievement of a sense of personal wholeness also catalyzes a self-transcending movement, in which fulfillment of self, paradoxically, is realized to involve transcendence of self.

Maslow (1970) described this process as self-actualization leading to self-transcendence. In his studies of highly self-actualizing people, he found that many described peak experiences, which are occasions of deep introspective insight, loving rapport with others, or profound religious revelations involving a sense that the ordinary physical and socially-defined limits of the self were transcended. Awareness of oneness with others, the universe, or the divine blossomed. These mystical experiences are often perceived as pivotal life moments that generate a powerful transformational shift of perspective and life style beyond egoism.

According to transpersonal and mystical perspectives, as unitive self-understanding grows, the implications for relations with other people and the world are inescapable. The person who grows to trans-egoic awareness begins to realize that one's own well-being and the well-being of all others are connected inextricably. If I am truly at one with you, then my joy and suffering are linked inextricably with your joy and suffering. Therefore, the self-transcending person becomes guided by a moral imperative that the search for one's own well-being should be linked to a compassionate commitment to support others' well-being. Thus, solutions to problems are sought from a win/win perspective in which all affected beings, human and nonhuman, are enhanced. Self-fulfillment, social justice, and the welfare of the entire planetary ecosystem are conjoined. A Buddhist metaphor for this is called Indra's Net (Macy, 1988). In this metaphor, the entire universe is imaged as the net of the god Indra. Every being is a precious jewel at a point of intersection between the strands of the net. All beings are interconnected within the net. And every jewel-like being reflects the resplendence of every other being.

Social work's service mission could be given great profundity by operating from such a spiritually expansive perspective. First of all, social workers would be cognizant of the inherent spiritual potential in every client and themselves. Even when starting with a client's goals for physical support, this itself would be understood as an aspect of a spiritual journey. Each client would be regarded as a precious jewel, a reflection of this divine resplendence. Within a Christian belief context, for example, every person we help can be perceived as Christ, especially those who are oppressed, impoverished, or desperately ill. The last line of an important prayer in Mother Teresa's religious order is that, as members serve others, they may recognize Christ "in the distressing disguise of the Poorest of the Poor" (Vardey, 1995, p. xxvi).

People who wish to explore the transpersonal reaches of their potential could also be assisted by social workers, who are in an especially appropriate position to help clients reflect on the interplay between inner spiritual growth and responsibility to society and nature, given our person-in-environment focus. Plans to assist and advocate for clients then would take into account the impact of any changes on other people, including people who may be in conflict with the client. In summary, a spiritually sensitive understanding of human fulfillment links personal growth, social justice, and ecojustice. This presents a tremendous opportunity for professional theories and practice strategies to go beyond a goal of egoistic self-actualization to a goal of mutual benefit for all beings.

HUMAN DIVERSITY

As Russel pointed out, the Council on Social Work Education's curriculum policy guidelines note that spiritual and religious diversity should be addressed along with other forms of human diversity. This raises the challenge of how social workers can honor the diverse and even conflicting religious and nonreligious expressions of spirituality. How can we respond supportively and competently to the incredible range of spiritual perspectives, while remaining faithful to our own spiritual commitments?

At a minimum, social workers need to be educated to be respectful and knowledgeable about spiritual diversity. The educational efforts that Russel documents are crucial. But spiritually-competent practice, just like culturally-competent practice, needs to go beyond mere tolerance and knowledge to appreciation and proactive ecumenism, interreligious dialogue, and universalistic spiritual awareness. A model for transcultural understanding can be helpful here (Canda, Carrizosa, and Yellow Bird, 1995). This model suggests three creative options for intercultural competence: biculturality, multiculturality, and transculturality. By extension, we can consider analogous options for relating across differences between spiritual perspectives.

A person who has achieved bicultural spiritual competence would be knowledgeable, comfortable, and skillful interacting within two different spiritual perspectives, such as atheist and fundamentalist Christian. This would require that the social worker has a clear awareness of his or her own spiritual beliefs and commitments, so that confusion and disorientation do not overwhelm the person when interacting with people of different or even conflicting views. Further, this realistically can be achieved through an overarching spiritual framework that can encompass respectfully both spiritual perspectives. This challenge is compounded when a person seeks to develop competence relating across many spiritual perspectives. For example, multicultural spirituality would involve the ability to relate across atheistic, theistic, agnostic, animistic, nontheistic, and polytheistic perspectives. Since people within each of these perspectives may claim ultimate truth for their beliefs, conflict and confusion might arise for the social worker who connects across them. However, such spiritual flexibility and comprehensive understanding would be necessary for the social worker to serve as a bridge, mediator, and creative integrator between spiritual perspectives.

The attempt to accomplish this raises a powerful existential question: Is there a Truth that embraces all these disparate claims of truth, honoring them in their distinctness while linking them in their commonality? Such a possibility is suggested by the concept of transculturality. A transcultural spiritual perspective would embrace diversity and commonality. Transcultural spirituality goes to the heart or center of what it is to be a human being. When we "center" ourselves, we come to a clear awareness of who we are most deeply and fundamentally, before and beyond cultural constructions, social roles, and personal idiosyncrasies. We discover that our own true nature involves a common-heartedness with all others. We realize that all people are on a spiritual search for meaning. In keeping with the value of mutual benefit, we realize that we all need to support each other in this quest. When our disagreements and differences about truth encounter each other in a respectful way, open to learning and expansion of understanding, we can all enhance each other.

This is a very sophisticated form of spirituality. Social work educators and practitioners need to explore how such a comprehensive and compassionate mode of awareness and action can be encouraged. The work of Fowler (1981) on faith development suggests that a universalizing faith or spirituality develops through a continuous growth process of working through spiritual ambiguities, questions, and confrontations. It seems crucial, therefore, that social work education and training address students' development beyond the teaching of knowledge or skills, and include mentoring for spiritual discernment, deep personal introspection, and active dialogue and cooperation across spiritual perspectives.

SELF-DETERMINATION

As previously discussed, transpersonal theory suggests a concept of the self that is interdependent and united with others. An expanded concept of self-determination follows from this. If the self is not an isolated or autonomous thing, then self-determination must imply other-determination as well. Freedom to determine one's own life goals, morals, and spiritual perspective implies responsibility to support other people's freedom and efforts to do the same. Realization of the complementarity of freedom and responsibility conveys a standard of mutuality. Freedom is a dynamic, transactional process, not merely a matter of formal rights or legal injunctions.

Social workers need to explore the implications of this in order to move beyond ego-centered understandings of self-actualization and self-determination (Siporin, 1985). Universalistic spirituality does not afford simplistic positions of either moral relativism ("anything goes") or moral absolutism ("my way is the only way"). An interdependent understanding of self does not allow either self-centeredness or self-abnegation. The implications of this for the Code of Ethics need to be considered.

For example, as Ressler discusses, our religiously pluralistic society raises many dilemmas about freedom to practice religion versus separation between church and state. As social workers then we need to engage in direct practice and political activities that are spiritually inclusive, even inclusive of exclusivist religious positions (Canda and Chambers, 1993). We need to develop ways to engage in critical reflection about the possible harmful and helpful aspects of religious participation without falling into pejorative assumptions about spiritual traditions very different from our own, even those we may prejudicially label as cults or fundamentalist sects (Lewandowski and Canda, 1995). We can encourage client self-determination in the context of moral reflection about the implications of clients' choices for other people and nonhuman beings. Further, we can support the rights of spiritual traditions and communities, as well as individuals, to be self-determining.

PERSON-IN-ENVIRONMENT

Koenig and Spano use Taoist philosophy to explain that reality cannot be broken down into chunks without violating it. There is a holistic quality inherent in all systems, hence, the social work dictum 'to work with person-in-environment transactions.' However, consideration of spirituality exposes three common gaps in professional discussions of the person and the environment.

First, the person is usually conceived in a narrow individualistic ego-bounded manner. Most social work based discussions of the person ignore the spiritual and transpersonal aspects, as Carroll pointed out. In order to correct this, social work needs to examine the implications of transpersonal theory for an interdependent and trans-egoic understanding of personhood.

Second, the environment is usually conceived in a narrow sense of the social environment, particularly a rather small extent of an individual client's social environment, such as family and direct support systems (Robbins, Chatterjee, and Canda, in press). At least in the curricula, we attempt to show the links between micro, meso, and macro levels of human behavior, practice, research, and policy. Yet an international perspective on the global human community, geopolitics, and social justice is not a standard component of our education. We do not address international responsibilities of the profession in the NASW Code of Ethics. The imperative for compassionate action deriving from mature spirituality calls us to examine nonviolent strategies and models for social development that uplift all people in all cultures, such as those proposed by Mahatma Gandhi (Sharma, 1987) and the Buddhist Sarvodaya Shramadana movement (Macy, 1991).

The total planetary ecology, including the web of all human and nonhuman beings, is even more rarely addressed in social work than the global human community (Hoff and McNutt, 1994). Social service agencies rarely have systematic policies, programs, and procedures taking into account the damaging effects of our social interventions on the natural ecology. The gigantic quantities of waste paper and computer equipment discarded by agencies is only one example of the way we may be destroying the planet upon which we all depend for life in the process of trying to help people to live.

The third gap in common understanding of the person-environment relationship is revealed by transpersonal and mystical insights about the fundamental interconnectedness and unity among all things. It is not merely the case that person and environment are inter-connected. Even further, the person and the environment are not separable. The metaphor of Indra's Net, mentioned previously, suggests that we need to revision the person-in-environment concept in a dramatic way. The rapidly expanding field of deep ecology could provide many insights for social work to explore in this regard (Sessions, 1995).

THE HELPING RELATIONSHIP

The authors in this volume have already indicated many implications for the development of particular practice skills and techniques. A spiritually-sensitive approach to practice would apply these skills and techniques within the context of a particular kind of helping relationship. A spiritually-sensitive relationship recognizes the inherent dignity and worth of the client, regardless of beliefs and behaviors. The client does not need to earn or deserve this respect. People merit respect simply on the basis of their being. As the Jewish existentialist theologian Martin Buber put it, the humane relationship is one of I to Thou, that is, subject to subject, full person to full person (Imre, 1971). If social workers reduce clients to diagnostic labels, clients are stripped of their full humanity. A person who becomes perceived as a "borderline," rather than a person with borderline personality disorder, for example, is treated merely as a stereotype of a psychiatric disorder. The person's strengths and resources, joys and struggles, aspirations and personal quirks are all obscured.

I-Thou relationship is developed through dialogue and mutual discovery between worker and client, as Early demonstrated through her interactios with Brent. As Koenig and Spano indicated, the strengths perspective is conducive to spiritually-sensitive practice because it honors the client as the expert in his or her own life. The social worker is a collaborator, facilitator, and fellow pilgrim with the client. Both learn and grow through the helping relationship.

Spiritually-sensitive practice gives a deepened meaning to empathy. Expression of empathy does involve skills of accurate listening, critical reflection, and appropriate feedback to the client. However, empathy cannot be reduced to skills or techniques. An insincere statement of "It seems like you feel . . . , because . . ." can easily be recognized as fakery by clients. Even a computer can be programmed to reiterate statements of feelings by clients. But only a person can intuitively connect with another, sensing the person's inner feelings, anticipating the implications, and gaining insight into the right response just at that particular moment. Luoma and Koenig and Spano point out that an intuitive connection is central to practice wisdom. Social work education needs to pay more attention to helping social workers enhance their capacity for empathy and intuition, for example, through mindfulness meditation (Keefe, 1986). Social work agencies need to consider how to make the work environment and schedules more conducive to empathy, allowing time and peaceful space for workers and clients to recollect themselves, to reflect, and to communicate with a sense of the sacredness of the relationship.

CONCLUSION

This essay suggests that when social work is infused with spirituality, promoting human fulfillment can become a process that creatively connects personal growth, social justice, and ecojustice. When social workers relate across spiritual diversity, we are challenged to quest for a mode of awareness and communication that embraces all varieties of religious and spiritual perspectives. When we advocate for individual and collective self-determination we confront questions pertaining to moral responsibility and tolerance of conflicting beliefs. As social work expands its understanding of person-environment transaction, it is challenged to go beyond egocentrism, nationalism, and human-centeredness. When the helping relationship reflects genuine respect and empathy, we deepen our awareness of the inherent sacredness of each person and each helping situation.

Although this essay has suggested many possibilities for continuing innovation by linking spirituality to social work, more questions, quandaries, possibilities and challenges are offered than answers. Even the answers are meant to be tentative, exploratory, and provisional. The profession of social work is now reclaiming its heritage of spirituality. But it is doing this with a significant question that was not paramount in the minds of the religious founders of the profession. That is: How can we address spirituality, not only from particular sectarian belief systems but also from a perspective that honors and embraces spiritual diversity? This is the fundamental question underlying all the others raised in this essay. As we continue the innovative work exhibited in this volume, we may sometimes be unsure of answers, but we will never go far wrong if we remember this question.

REFERENCES

Canda, E. R., Carrizosa, S., and Yellow Bird, M. (1995). *Cultural diversity in child welfare practice: A Training Curriculum for Cultural Competence.* Lawrence, KS: The University of Kansas School of Social Welfare.

Canda, E. R. and Chambers, D. (1993). Should spiritual principles guide social policy? Yes. In Howard J. Karger and James Midgely, Eds., *Controversial Issues in Social Policy.* Boston: Allyn and Bacon, pp. 63-78.

Fowler, J. (1981). *Stages of faith: The psychology of human development and the quest for meaning.* New York: Harper and Row.

Hoff, M. and McNutt, J. G. (Eds.). (1994). *The global environmental crisis: Implications for social welfare and social work.* Brookefield, VT: Avebury.

Imre, R. (1971). A theological view of social casework. *Social Casework, 52*(9), 578-585.

Keefe, T. (1986). Meditation and social work treatment. In F. J. Turner, Ed., *Social Work Treatment: Interlocking Theoretical Approaches*, third edition. New York: Free Press, pp. 155-180.

Lewandowski, C. A. and Canda, E. R. (1995). A typological model for assessment of religious groups. *Social Thought, 18* (1), 17-38.

Macy, J. (1991). *World as lover, world as self.* Berkeley: Parallax Press.

Macy, J. (1988). In Indra's net: Sarvodaya and our mutual efforts for peace. In

Fred Eppsteiner, Ed., *The Path of Compassion: Writings on Socially Engaged Buddhism*, Berkeley: Parallax Press, pp. 170-181.

Maslow, A. H. (1970). *Religions, values, and peak experiences.* New York: Viking.

Robbins, S., Chatterjee, P., and Canda, E. R. (in press). *Contemporary human behavior theory: A critical perspective for social work.* Boston: Allyn and Bacon.

Sessions, G., Ed. (1995). *Deep ecology for the 21st Century.* Boston: Shamhala.

Sharma, S. (1987). Development, peace, and nonviolent social change: The Gandhian perspective. *Social Development Issues, 10* (3), 31-45.

Siporin, M. (1985). Current social work perspectives on clinical practice. *Clinical Social Work Journal, 13* (3), 198-217.

Vardey, L., Ed. (1995). *Mother Teresa: A simple path.* New York: Ballantine Books.

Wilber, K. (1995). *Sex, ecology, spirituality: The spirit of evolution.* Boston: Shambhala.

Index

Accreditation issues,16,18,25
Adolescence, psychospiritual crisis
    of death
    barriers for social workers, 67-68
    case study, 68-74
    diagnosis, 70-71
    dreams, 71-73
    metaphors, 69-70
    spiritual development, 74-75
    transpersonal theory, 75-79
    unfinished business, 73-74
Afterlife, 72-74,77-79
Age, in psychosocial distress about
    death, 76
Agor, W., 34
Alcoholism. *See* Substance abuse
    and controlled substances
All-at-one-time knowledge in
    Taoism, 57-60
American Jurisprudence, 85-86
Animal sacrifice, 90
Atheism, 2-3
Axline, Virginia, 55

Baby boomers, interest in
    spirituality, 17-18
Beliefs. *See* Values
Biology, intuition in, 35
Biopsychosocial model, 4,52
Bipolar disorder, 53-54
Buddhism, 2-3,52,99
Business theory, intuition in, 34

Cancer, 67-80
Canda, Edward, 2-3,7,68,75

Cantwell v. Connecticut, 87
Carter, S., 92
Childhood trauma, student survivors
    of, 26
Christianity, 99
    conceptualization of spirituality,
    2-3
    original sin, 52
Chuang Tzu, 60
Church of the Lukumi Babalu Aye v.
    City of Hialeah, 90
Church/state relationship, 81-95
    complexity, 82-84
    court cases, 84-90
    implications for social work,
    92-93
    models, 91-92
Collaboration, 50
Constitution, The, 83,86-87
Coping mechanisms, 74
Council on Social Work Education,
    16,18,25
Court cases, 84-92
Cowley, A. S., 36
Crisis
    as danger and opportunity, 8,9
    psychospiritual crisis of dying
    adolescent, 67-80
Cultural issues, 85
*Culture of Disbelief: How American
    Law and Politics Trivialize
Religious Devotion, The,* (Carter), 92
Curriculum development, for
    graduate spirituality
    courses, 21-23,25-26,27

Dass, R., 23
Death, psychospiritual crisis of dying
    adolescent, 67-80
    barriers for social workers, 67-68
    case study, 68-74
    diagnosis, 70-71
    dreams, 71-73
    metaphors, 69-70
    spiritual development, 74-75
    transpersonal theory, 75-79
    unfinished business, 73-74
Decision making, 58,61-62
Derezotes, D., 36
Development of spirituality, 101
    adolescence and death, 74-79
    essence and dimension, 6-7,10
Disassociative symptoms, 53
Disidentification in death, 78-79
Diversity issues, 19,24,26,100-101
Dreams, 71-73,77-79
Dysfunctional behavior, views of, 8-11

Economic issues, 82-84
Education. *See also* Graduate school
    education
    intuition in theories of, 33-34
    legal issues, 88
    student perceptions of intuition,
        37-43
Educators. *See* Faculty
Emotion management, 74
Empathy, 104
Employment Division v. Smith,
    89-90
Empowerment, 50
Engel v. Vitale, 88
Establishment Clause, 87,88
Everson v. Board of Education, 87-88
Evil in Taoism, 52
Existentialism
    conceptualization of spirituality,
        2-3
    self-actualization, 6,75-76,99

Faculty
    attitudes and instruction in
        graduate spirituality
        courses, 23-26
    colleague resistance, 23
    survey of attitudes toward
        spirituality, 18-19
Family, of dying adolescent, 69,73,
    74,76-77
Family Research Council, 85
First Amendment, 83,86-87
Frankel, Victor, 53
Full Spectrum Model (Wilber), 36
Funding issues, 82-84

Good and evil in Taoism, 52
Gorman, P., 23
Graduate school education,
        spirituality in, 15-29
    current status, 18-19
    diversity issues, 24,26
    faculty attitudes and instruction,
        23-26
    literature review, 16-20
    reasons for including, 18
    student evaluations, 24
    survey of, 20-26
    teaching methods, 24,26
    texts, 23,26
    topics, 19-20,21-23, 25-26

Health/healing, in social work
        paradigm, 3-4
Heaven, 72-74,77-79
Heraclitus, 49
"High and impregnable" standard,
    88-89
Holistic dualism, 51-54
Housing and Urban Development
        (HUD) Department, 84,89
How Can I Help? (Dass and
        Gorman), 23
Huai Nan Tzu, 50-51

HUD, 84,89
Human fulfillment, 98-100

Illinois, 88
Individuation, 6
Indra's Net, 99
Institute of Noetic Sciences, 34
Interconnectedness. *See*
        Relationships and
        spirituality
Intuition
    in practice and education, 31-45,
        104
        literature review, 32-37
        student perceptions of, 37-43
        terminology, 32
    in Taoism, 57-60
Intuition Network, 34
I-Thou relationship, 104

Johanson, G., 55,61
Judaism, 2-3
Jung, C., 6,7,33

Knowing-in-action, 59
Knowledge, in strengths perspective,
        58-60
Kurtz, R., 55,61

Language, Taoism perspective on, 49
Lao Tzu, 51,54,61
Lee, F., 91-92
Legal issues in church/state
        relationship, 81-95
    complexity, 82-84
    court cases, 84-90
    implications for social work,
        92-93
    models, 91-92
Lemon test, 88-89

Lemon v. Kurtzman, 88-89
Linear thinking, 57
Loewenberg, F. M., 23
Logotherapy, 53
Louisiana, 86
Lovinger, R. J., 23

McCollum v. Board of Education, 88
Medical model, 52-53
Medicine, intuition in, 35
Mindfulness, 56
Mississippi, 84-85
Moral education theory, intuition in, 34
Moral issues, 85,102
Mother, separation from, 69,73-74,
        76-77
M.S.W. curriculum. *See* Graduate
        school education
Myers-Briggs Type Indicator, 33
Mystical experiences, 99

Native Americans, 89-90
Nebraska, 86
New York State, 88
Noddings, N., 33
Nonaction in Taoism, 54-57
Normalization of death, 76-77
Nursing home placement, 61-62

Oppression, Taoist view of, 56-57
Original sin, 52

Pennsylvania, 88
Personal Responsibility and Work
        Opportunity Act of 1996,
        81-82
Person-in-environment, 102-103
Peter Pan metaphor, 69
Peyote, 89
Practice implications
    diversity issues, 100-101

helping relationships, 103-104
human fulfillment, 98-100
legal issues in church/state
    relationship, 92-93
person-in-environment, 102-103
psychospiritual crisis of dying
    adolescent, 67-68,75
self-determination, 101-102
spiritual as essence and
    dimension, 8-11
survey of attitudes toward
    spirituality, 18-19
of Taoism
    all-at-one-time knowledge, 58-59
    holistic dualism, 53-54
    nonaction, 55-57
    reality as process, 50-51
    virtue, 61-63
Practice wisdom, intuition in, 35-37
Prayer in public schools, 88
Proactive in transegoic model, 78
Psychology, intuition, 33

Qualitative changes,
        spirituality-as-essence, 7
Quantitative changes,
        spirituality-as-dimension, 7
Quantum physics, intuition in, 35

Reagan administration, 82
Reality as process in Taoism, 49-51
Reframing, 8
Relationships and spirituality
    essence and dimension
        practice implications, 8-11
        theoretical implications, 5
    helping relationship, 103-104
    person-in-environment, 102-103
    social work theory, 4
    transpersonal theory, 33,35-36,
        75-79,8-100

Religion. *See also* Church/state
        relationship
    in adolescence, 77
    vs. spirituality, 2, 17
*Religion and Counseling: The
        Psychological Impact of
        Religious Belief* (Lovinger),
        23
*Religion and Social Work Practice in
        Contemporary American
        Society* (Loewenberg), 23
Religious Freedom Restoration Act
        in 1993, 90
Religious institutions in social
        service, 82-84,85
Religious instruction in schools, 88
Research issues, graduate spirituality
        courses, 27
Rhode Island, 88
Richmond, M., 6
Rosenberger v. Rector and Visitors of
        University of Virginia, 89

Salvation Army, 83-84
Santeria church, 90
Schools
    prayer in, 88
    religious instruction in, 88
    transportation to sectarian, 88
Self-actualization, 6,75-76,99
Self-awareness, in Taoism, 60-63
Self-determination, 101-102
Self-development and transformation
    in adolescence, 75-76
    spirituality as essence and
        dimension, 4-5,6-7
    transpersonal theory, 33,35-36,
        75-79,98-100
Sermabeikian, P., 75
Sexual abuse, holistic dualism in
        treatment, 53-54
Shamanism, conceptualization of
        spirituality, 2-3
Sherbert v. Verner, 90
Social action, client-driven, 56-57

Social service funding, 82-84
Social work practice. *See* Practice
    implications
Sore, P., 33
Spencer, S. W., 16
Spirituality
    conceptualization of, 1-13
        developmental issues, 6-7
        essence and dimension, 2-5,
            8-11
        practice implications, 8-11
        relationships and, 5
        terminology, 2
        theoretical implications, 5-7
    in graduate school education,
        15-29
        literature review, 16-20
        survey of, 20-26
    public interest in, 17-18
    terminology, 17
Statistical analysis, 38
Strengths perspective, 48,50,52-53,
    55-57,58-59,62-63
Student evaluations, of graduate
    spirituality courses, 24
Students
    perceptions of intuition, 37-43
    survey of attitudes toward
        spirituality, 18-19
    survivors of childhood trauma, 26
Substance abuse and controlled
        substances
    legal issues, 89-90
    religious organizations in
        treatment, 85
    spirituality in treatment, 8, 11
Supreme Court cases, 85-92

Taoism, 47-65
    all-at-one-time knowledge, 57-60
    holistic dualism and practice,
        51-54
    literature parallels, 63-64
    nonaction, 54-57

    principles of, 48-49
    reality as process, 49-51
    strengths perspective and, 48,53
    virtue, 60-63
Tao te Ching, 51
Tau-b value, 38,41
Teaching methods, in graduate
    spirualtiy courses, 24,26
Teen Challenge, 85
Te in Taoism, 60-63
Texts, for graduate spirituality
    courses, 23,26
Theistic humanism, 2-3
Therapeutic relationship. *See*
    Practice implications
Transcendence in spirituality, 5,9,10,
    75, 99
Transcultural model, 100-101
Transegoic model. *See* Transpersonal
    theory
Transpersonal theory, 33,35-36,
    75-79,98-100
Transrational in intuition, 35-36
Treatment. *See* Practice implications
Treatment modalities, spirituality as
    essence and dimension, 8-9,
    10,11
Turtle defense, 69
Twelve-step programs, 11

Unconscious knowledge in Taoism,
    57-60
University of Virginia, 89

Values
    practice implications, 10
    in Taoism, 51
Virtue in Taoism, 60-63

Washington, D.C., 84
Watts, Alan W., 57-58
Weick, A., 3-4

Welfare reform, 82-84
Western tradition, assumptions and
        limitations, 48
"What's Up Ministries," 85
Wholeness, spirituality as essence
        and dimension, 7
Wilber, Ken, 33,36
WORD-UP Youth Outreach, 85
Wu wei in Taoism, 54-57

Zen Buddhism, 52

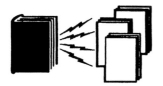

Haworth
DOCUMENT DELIVERY
SERVICE

This valuable service provides a single-article order form for any article from a Haworth journal.

- *Time Saving:* No running around from library to library to find a specific article.
- *Cost Effective:* All costs are kept down to a minimum.
- *Fast Delivery:* Choose from several options, including same-day FAX.
- *No Copyright Hassles:* You will be supplied by the original publisher.
- *Easy Payment:* Choose from several easy payment methods.

Open Accounts Welcome for . . .
- Library Interlibrary Loan Departments
- Library Network/Consortia Wishing to Provide Single-Article Services
- Indexing/Abstracting Services with Single Article Provision Services
- Document Provision Brokers and Freelance Information Service Providers

---

MAIL or *FAX* THIS ENTIRE ORDER FORM TO:

Haworth Document Delivery Service
The Haworth Press, Inc.
10 Alice Street
Binghamton, NY 13904-1580

or FAX: 1-800-895-0582
or CALL: 1-800-342-9678
9am-5pm EST

PLEASE SEND ME PHOTOCOPIES OF THE FOLLOWING SINGLE ARTICLES:
1) Journal Title: _____
    Vol/Issue/Year:_____Starting & Ending Pages:_____
Article Title:_____
_____

2) Journal Title: _____
    Vol/Issue/Year:_____Starting & Ending Pages:_____
Article Title:_____
_____

3) Journal Title: _____
    Vol/Issue/Year:_____Starting & Ending Pages:_____
Article Title:_____
_____

4) Journal Title: _____
    Vol/Issue/Year:_____Starting & Ending Pages:_____
Article Title:_____
_____

(See other side for Costs and Payment Information)

COSTS: Please figure your cost to order quality copies of an article.

1. Set-up charge per article: $8.00
   ($8.00 × number of separate articles) _____

2. Photocopying charge for each article:

   1-10 pages: $1.00 _____

   11-19 pages: $3.00 _____

   20-29 pages: $5.00 _____

   30+ pages: $2.00/10 pages _____

3. Flexicover (optional): $2.00/article _____

4. Postage & Handling: US: $1.00 for the first article/
   $.50 each additional article _____

   Federal Express: $25.00 _____

   Outside US: $2.00 for first article/
   $.50 each additional article _____

5. Same-day FAX service: $.35 per page _____

   GRAND TOTAL: _____

METHOD OF PAYMENT: (please check one)

❑ Check enclosed   ❑ Please ship and bill. PO # _____
(sorry we can ship and bill to bookstores only! All others must pre-pay)

❑ Charge to my credit card: ❑ Visa; ❑ MasterCard; ❑ Discover;
❑ American Express;

Account Number:_____ Expiration date:_____

Signature: ✗_____

Name: _____ Institution: _____

Address: _____

_____

City: _____ State:_____ Zip:_____

Phone Number: _____ FAX Number: _____

MAIL or *FAX* THIS ENTIRE ORDER FORM TO:

Haworth Document Delivery Service
The Haworth Press, Inc.
10 Alice Street
Binghamton, NY 13904-1580

or **FAX:** 1-800-895-0582
or **CALL:** 1-800-342-9678
9am-5pm EST)